Frank Werny

Hike Plyr
Great Walks among the Pines and Ponds of
By Frank Werny

MW00595573

Cranberry Bogs off Lout Pond Road

Over 70 Hikes in and around the Plymouth, MA, Area

1

Frank Werny

Hike Plymouth!
Over 70 Great Walks among the Pines and Ponds of Plymouth, MA
By Frank Werny

Disclaimer
As in other hiking books, the information in this book is meant as a guide only. The author cannot be responsible for the conditions of the trails, for the safety of the trails, the accuracy of the maps, for anything that happens while you are using the trails, or for the continued accessibility of the trails. The introduction includes some advice, but following that advice also is not sufficient to guarantee a safe hike or walk. Use common sense, make adequate preparations, and take proper precautions during the hike.

Printed in the United States of America
Published by On Blueberry Hill Press
First Edition 2011

Text by Frank Werny
Cover Design by Cover Creator and Frank Werny
All photos and trail maps by Frank Werny unless otherwise noted
Cover photo taken at eastern corner of Great Island Pond

Library of Congress Control Number 2011905315
ISBN-13: 978-1461037156
ISBN-10: 1461037158

Please direct comments or corrections to frankwerny@gmail.com

On Blueberry Hill Press
Plymouth, MA
frankwerny@gmail.com

Frank Werny

Hike Plymouth!
By Frank Werny

Acknowledgements
I would like to again acknowledge my wife's patience with my interest in hiking and thank her for her company in scouting many of the hikes. I would also like to thank my friend, Chuck Harper, who scouted and hiked most of the hikes with me over the last 7 years. My thanks also go to my more recent scouting buddies Carl Ojala and Dick Terry, and the people in my hiking group for trying the hikes with me.

Dedication
This book is dedicated to our sons, Mark, Scott, Chris, Todd, and Tim, and their families. They are leading active and productive lives and we are proud of them.

Additional books are available at www.createspace.com/3586892
Or frankwerny@gmail.com or www.amazon.com

Similar books available by the author:
'Great Walks Among the Pines and Ponds of Plymouth and Surrounding Areas'.
50 easy hikes in and around the Plymouth, MA, area. Full color.
www.createspace.com/3399738

'Walks among the Pines and Ponds of Plymouth and Surrounding Areas'.
Over 70 easy hikes in and around the Plymouth, MA, area. Black and white.
www.createspace.com/3380596

To facilitate printing of individual instructions and trail maps, copies of the book are available on CD from frankwerny@gmail.com

3

Frank Werny

Table of Contents

Table of Hikes

Hike	Off	mi	Time	Features	Page
Center Hill Conservation Area	3A	2.6	1:20	B, Bg, Pi, Po	97
Ellisville Harbor	3A	2.4	1:00	B, Pi, V	99
R. F. Wynn Reservation	3A	2.4	1:05	Bg, Pi, Po	101
Sagamore Hill, Cape Cod Canal	3A	5	1:55	B, Pi, V	103
Agawam Road to Fawn Pond	LPR	3.6	1:30	Bg, Pi, Po, R	66
Around Halfway Pound	LPR	3.5	1:30	Bg, Pi, Po	63
Between Clark Rd & PSHS	LPR	2.8	1:20	Pi, Po	55
Bloody Pond	LPR	3.2	1:45	Pi, Po	65
Boot Pond	LPR	2.5	1:00	PI, Po	52
Gramp's Loop	LPR	2	0:55	Pi	61
Halfway Pond Area	LPR	2	1:00	Pi, Po	59
Hedges Pond	LPR	1.6	0:45	Pi, Po	73
Hoyts Pond, Eel River Preserve	LPR	2	1:10	Bg, Pi, Po, R	50
Makepeace Bogs	LPR	2.7	1:40	Bg, R	69
Pickerel Pond	LPR	2.6	1:20	Bg, Pi, Po	76
Russell Mill Pond	LPR	4.4	2:50	Pi, Po, R	47
Six Ponds Cons. Area East	LPR	3	1:00	Pi	57
White Island Bogs	LPR	3.4	1:25	Bg, Pi, Po	71
Around College Pond	MS	5.1	2:00	Pi, Po	79
Central Forest & Fire Tower	MS	4.2	1:30	Pi, V	84
Charge and Fearing Pond	MS	4.8	1:45	Pi, Po	81
East Entrance Trail	MS	3.1	1:45	Pi	85
East Head Reserv. from Headq.	MS	2.6	1:10	Pi, Po	87
East Head Reservoir from P2	MS	5.2	2:15	Pi, Po	88
Federal & Rocky Ponds	MS	5.2	0:00	Bg, Pi, Po	90
Lost Horse Bog	MS	5.2	0:00	Bg, Pi	92
Three Cornered Pond	MS	4.1	1:40	Pi, Po	94
Bay Farm & Mulliken's Landing	NP	2.9	1:20	B, Pi, R	138
Camp Wing	NP	1.7	0:45	Pi, PO, R	140
Duxbury Beach	NP	8	2:30	B, V	143
Duxbury Bogs	NP	2.3	1:00	Bg, Pi	146
Lansing-Bennett Forest	NP	2.1	0:00	Pi, Po, R	148
North Hill Marsh Area	NP	2.9	1:15	Bg, Pi, Po	152
O. W. Steward Preserve	NP	1.5	1:00	Pi, Po	157
Round Pond Conservation Area	NP	3.4	12:00	Bg, Pi, Po	154
Tucker Preserve	NP	3.4	1:20	Pi, Po, R	160
Willow Brook Farm Preserve	NP	3	1:15	Pi, R	164
Over Manomet Hill & S. Ridge	OS	3.3	1:30	Bg, Pi	25
Around Old Sandwich Club	OS	4.3	1:45	Bg, Pi, Po	31
Bog and Pond of The Pinehills	OS	2	1:10	Bg, Pi, Po	33
Cathedral Rd over Manomet Hill	OS	4.7	2:00	PI, V	18

7

Cathedral Road	OS	2.6	1:00	Pi	15
Cleft Rock via Manomet Hill	OS	5.4	1:55	Pi, R, V	16
Four Ponds (Manomet)	OS	4.6	1:40	Bg, Pi, Po,	39
Hathaway Pond	OS	2.8	1:20	Bg, Pi, Po	41
Morey Hole-Briggs Reservoir	OS	4.2	1:50	Bg, Pi, Po	43
Fire Tower and Manomet Hill	OS	4.1	1:55	Pi, V	19
Fire tower; Ridge Overlook	OS	3.9	2:00	Pi, V	21
South Ridge	OS	3.6	1:25	PI, V	26
Talcott Parcel	OS	3.7	1:40	Pi, Po	45
The Pinehills South	OS	4.9	2:10	Pi	35
West PH, Bog, Winslow's View	OS	3.2	1:05	Bg, Pi, Po	37
Crawley Woodlands Preserve	P	2.5	1:15	Pi, Po	127
Morton Park Ponds	P	3.2	1:35	Pi, Po	122
Plymouth Long Beach	P	6.2	2:15	B, V	129
Rock to Billington Sea	P	4	1:40	Pi, Po, R	124
Plymouth Rock to Cordage	P	3.8	1:30	B	119
Russell Saw Mill Pond	P	1.8	0:45	Pi, Po	118
Town Forest, Cooks Pond	P	3.5	1:20	Bg, Pi, Po	133
Town Forest, S. Triangle Pond	P	2.5	1:30	Pi, Po	134
Century Bog	P P	3.7	1:45	Bg, Pi	107
Horse Pond	P P	2	1:15	Pi, Po	111
Red Brook	P P	3.8	1:30	Bg, PI, R	113
Weeks Pond	P P	3.2	1:15	Bg, Pi, R	114
Carter Beal Preservation Area	SPH	2.5	1:20	Bg, Pi, Po	167
Bourne Farm	SPH	2.4	1:20	Bg, Pi, Po, R	169
C C Canal; Bournedale Hill	SPH	3.1	1:10	Pi, Canal	172
C C Canal; Sandwich Boardwlk	SPH	3.8	1:20	B, Pi	175
Four Pond Cons. Area (Bourne)	SPH	4.2	2:10	Pi, Po, R	177
Great Neck Cons. Area	SPH	3.9	1:45	Pi, Po, R	179
Lyman Conservation Area	SPH	2.8	1:40	B, Pi, R	182
Sandy Neck Beach	SPH	7.8	2:40	B	185
Scorton Creek	SPH	3.6	2:00	Pi, Po, R	186

Locations:
NP= North Of Plymouth; SPH= South of the Pine Hills; P=Town of Plymouth;
OS =Off Old Sandwich Road; MS = Myles Standish State Forest;
P P= Plymouth Parks Area; LPR=Off Long Pond Road; 3A= Off Rt. 3A
Features: B=Beach, Bg=Bog, Pi=Pines, Po=Ponds, R=River or Brook, V= View

Distribution Of All Hikes (Red lines are hikes)

Hike Plymouth!
By Frank Werny

Introduction

A. General

Over the last few years, since I arrived in Plymouth in 2003, I have taken a small group of people from The Pinehills on walks or short hikes in the Pine Hills and the surrounding areas about twice a month. Over several years of bi-monthly hikes, we were able to find many hikes in the 3 to 5 mile range. Some were as short as 2 miles and others were over 5 miles. The 365 ponds of Plymouth County, the pines, the hills, the bogs and the beaches are beautiful natural areas and generally accessible due to the diligent efforts of The Wildlands Trust, The Nature Conservancy, The Trustees of Reservations of MA, and the conservation efforts of the towns and others. We found over 70 hikes worth exploring, each offering its own unique setting, scenic features, and level of tranquility. We ventured as far north as Duxbury and as far south of the Pine Hills as Wareham and Sandwich on Cape Cod.

I do have to caution, Plymouth County is developing rapidly and despite the many conservation efforts, at some point in time, some roads and trails on the maps may no longer exist, and trails and roads may have changed, or may have been marked private or no trespassing. They were here in 2011 and most will be there for a while. We have hiked each of the hikes at least twice. We were careful and respectful as far as trespassing on properties that were not clearly marked 'Private' or 'No Trespassing'. Where we encountered owners they were friendly and provided us with local history and guidance. However, you have to use your own judgment when you encounter 'No Trespassing' or 'Private Road' signs. Many times these signs refer to land adjacent to the trails or paths. In general, we found that very few property owners objected if we respectfully just walked on a private road or stayed on existing trails when traversing areas marked 'No Trespassing''.

For each hike I included directions on how to get there and where to park, some of the key features of the hike, a few words to help you through the hike, a Google map of the area including the trail and some photos taken on hikes on that trail. Some trails are clearly marked with Wildlands Trust or town walking trail signs or colored markers on trees. Most are not marked at all. Although a hiking GPS or compass is not essential they can be useful.

Most of the hikes do not require more than a good pair of sneakers, and, of course, take water, especially in the summer. Please be aware of the danger of picking up ticks, deer ticks in particular, almost any time of year. Other insects are generally not a problem in the Plymouth area, but bring some insect repellant along just in case. Mosquitoes can be present in marshy areas.

Organizations

Several organizations are valuable resources for hiking as well as facilitating the conservation of the lands in and around Plymouth. They are, among others, The Wildlands Trust of Southeastern Massachusetts,

(www.wildlandstrust.org)[2], The Nature Conservancy
(www.nature.org/wherewework/northamerica/states/massachusetts/about/)[1]and
The Trustees of Reservations (www.ttor.org)[5]. The towns also, especially Plymouth,
Kingston, Wareham, Sandwich, Bourne, and Duxbury, are great resources for maps
and do conserve a lot of their land.

Resources:
The maps produced were prepared using a Garmin eTrex Venture HC GPS unit and
Garmin WayPoint and were overlaid on MassGiss maps[2] using the Google Earth
software. In addition some historical and location information was taken from
Wikipedia[4] on the internet.

Caution
I should also point out that due to ever changing conditions the author cannot be
responsible for the accuracy of the content of the book nor the safety of the trails.
You should use the book as a guide and always proceed with caution. Trails change,
weather conditions affect footing, ownership of the land changes etc.

1. Wildlands Trust of Southern Massachusetts, Po Box 2282, Duxbury, MA 02331
2. The Nature Conservancy, 205 Portland Street, Suite 400
Boston, MA 02114-1708
3. "Office of Geographic and Environmental Information (MassGiss), Commonwealth of
Massachusetts Executive Office of Environmental Affairs"
4. Wikipedia, http://wikipedia.org

11

II.   Off Old Sandwich Road

Old Sandwich Road is one of the oldest continually used roads in the country, established by the Pilgrims in 1642 and probably before that used by the local Indians to go to the Cape Cod area. Several hikes may be started from this road.

Wintry Old Sandwich Road

The hikes off Old Sandwich are divided into those on Manomet Hill and Ridge, The Pinehills, and others further south along Old Sandwich Road. Manomet Hill and Ridge, and The Pinehills are part of a region called The Pine Hills[4].It is a sparsely populated region located just south of Plymouth. It is mostly hilly and forested and lies south of Plymouth Beach and Chiltonville, west of Manomet, and on both sides of Route 3, where the southern portion of the region can be accessed from Exit 3 and the northern portion can be accessed from Exit 4. The area rises from Plymouth Bay at Rocky Point, which is located in the foothills of the region, and runs southwest. Route 3A winds through the heart of the Pine Hills. The region consists of the Rocky Point neighborhood in the northeast and *The Pinehills*, a new residential and commercial development in the southwestern part of the area[4].

Map of Hikes off Old Sandwich

A.   Manomet Hill

Manomet Hill is the highest peak in the Pine Hills. At 395 feet (120 m) above sea level, it is the highest point in Plymouth County. Several Trails criss-cross the hill. Some are shown on the map, but there are more and it pays to pay attention. There are 3 easy starting places off Old Sandwich Road for hikes or walks on Manomet Hill. By the Fire Tower Road, across from the OS Golf Club, from the Seaton Highlands community parking lot, and from the beginning of the future extension of Long Ridge Road.

13

A map of some of the trails on Manomet Hill and Ridge

Hikes north to south

        1.   **From Fire Tower Road entrance:**
        a) **Cathedral road**
        b) **Cleft Rock**
        c) **Cathedral Road over Manomet Hill and back**
        d) **Fire Tower and Manomet Hill**
        e) **Cathedral Road/Fire Tower/Ridge Outlook/SHL**

        2.   **From Seaton Highlands:**
        a) **Outlook/ Valley/ Fire Tower/SHL**
        b) **SHL/Outlook/Valley/SHL**
        c) **South Ridge**

        3.   **From Future Long Ridge Road Extension:**
        a) **Over South Ridge/Valley/ Back**

1.   **From Fire Tower Road entrance:**

a.   **Cathedral Road**

Directions and parking
Take Exit 3 from Hwy 3. Go east to Old Sandwich Road; turn left. This is a bumpy but wide dirt road for more than a mile. Go about two miles to the entrance of the Old Sandwich Club. Park across the street; on the east side of the road just north of the fire road. Be sure to leave access to the fire road open.
Approximate GPS street address: 248 Old Sandwich Rd, Plymouth, MA

Hike Difficulty
Very easy walk; 2.6 miles; no hills, soft pine needles and sandy trail

Features
Beautiful walk through the pines; Cathedral Road and Back Road. The land on either side of Back Road is private. However the east side is Entergy property and they do permit walking on their property between Back Road and Rt. 3A. Entergy Power Co (508 830-7000). You may confirm with Dave Tarantino (508 830-8895)

Hike
Start just north of the Fire Tower Road. The trail heads northeast, diagonally between the Fire Tower road and Old Sandwich Road. Continue straight across when you get to a junction of several trails. After you cross the power lines the trail, now Back Road, will head straight north. Continue on the trail till it dead ends almost on Doten Road. Turn around and walk back the same route.

Cathedral Road

Cathedral and Back Road

b. Cleft Rock via Manomet Hill

Directions and parking
Take Exit 3 from Hwy 3. Go east to Old Sandwich Road; turn left. This is a bumpy but wide dirt road for more than a mile. Go about two miles to the entrance of the Old Sandwich Club. Park across the street, on the east side of the road just north of the fire road. Be sure to leave access to the fire road open.
Approximate GPS street address: 248 Old Sandwich Rd, Plymouth, MA

Hike Difficulty
4.8 miles, 1:55 hr., gradual up and downs; easy walking.

Features:
Fire Tower; Pinehills Water Tank; long walk along ridge and then down to 3a; Manomet Hill Rotary (?);
Cleft Rock[4] is a rock formation located in the Pine Hills, known for the unique cleft that runs through its center. The rock formation is said to have been used as a lookout spot by the Native Americans, and it used to offer a panoramic view of Cape Cod Bay on a clear day. Trees are now in the way of a view. It is located in an 8.7-acre town park on Route 3A. It can also be reached by car on 3A.

16

Cleft Rock

The Hike

Start by walking up the fire road towards the fire tower. Pass by the water tank, and then pass by the road leading to the fire tower. Just past the road to the fire tower, there is a trail to the left/north. It is quite straight until you get to a rotary (top of Manomet Hill) and you take the trail exiting at 1 o'clock or northeast. Follow it until you get to Hwy 3A. Turn right and follow the busy highway about 500 feet to the entrance to Cleft Rock, a former city park, on the left. Return by retracing your steps.

Cleft Rock trail

17

c.   Cathedral Road over Manomet Hill and back

Directions
Take Exit 3 from Hwy 3. Go east to Old Sandwich Road; turn left. This is a bumpy but wide dirt road for more than a mile. Go about two miles to the entrance of the Old Sandwich Club. Park across the street, on the east side of the road just north of the fire road. Be sure to leave access to the fire road open.
Approximate GPS street address 248 Old Sandwich Rd, Plymouth, MA

Features
This is a hike up to and over Manomet Hill. Manomet Hill, Cathedral Road, Back Road. Much of the hike east of Cathedral Road is on Entergy Power Co (508 830-7000) land. They do not object to hiking on land west of 3A. You may confirm with Dave Tarantino (508 830-8895)

Difficulty
4.7 miles; about two hrs; two long up hills and down hills.

Hike
A few feet north of the fire tower road across from the Old Sandwich Golf Club entrance, the trail starts on Cathedral Road. It goes diagonally or northeast through the white pines. Follow Cathedral Road, also known as Back Road. You pass through one intersection of four trails and then get to the power lines. Cross over and continue on Cathedral Rd. After about ¼-mile pass up a gate on your right, go another ¼ mile plus till you see a trail on your right. Turn right onto Entergy land. Continue uphill for what will seem like a mile. Near the top stay right and emerge on Manomet Hill 'rotary'. Continue on the trail directly across the circle and to the right heading southeast. Continue downhill for about ½ mile and then look for a sharp right. Turn sharp right and head uphill. Notice the prevalence of deciduous trees vs. pines. Near the top stay, right and after a sharp left emerge on the trail that leads from Manomet Hill 'rotary' to the Fire Tower. Turn left. Continue for ~ ¼ mile. When the trail splits stay right and start heading downhill till you get to a gate and back to Cathedral Road. Turn left and follow it back out to the road and your car.

Cathedral/Back Road

Glacial Erratic

18

Cathedral Road over Manomet Hill and back

d.   Fire Tower and Manomet Hill

Directions and parking
Take Exit 3 from Hwy 3. Go east to Old Sandwich Road; turn left. This is a bumpy but wide dirt road for more than a mile. Go about two miles to the entrance of the Old Sandwich Club. Park across the street on the east side of the road, just north of the fire tower road. Be sure to leave access to the fire road open.
Approximate GPS street address 248 Old Sandwich Rd, Plymouth, MA

Hike Difficulty
3.7 miles; 1:25 hrs; gradual up and down hills.

Features:
The Pinehills Water Reservoir; State Fire Tower; View of Manomet beaches; Walk along Manomet Hill ridge.
Manomet Hill is the highest peak in the Pine Hills at 395 feet above sea level; it is the highest point in Plymouth.

Plymouth Tower

19

Height above sea level: 350 FT
Tower Structure Height: 78 FT
First date of operation: 1969

Cape Cod Bay from Manomet Hill

Fire Tower 2008

ca.1908

ca.1940

ca. 1908 from a postcard supplied Eleanor Tillinghast.
ca. 1940 from:
http://www.jabezcorner.com/Vanished%20Plymouth/pine_hills_tower.htm

The Hike
The whole hike is on Pine Hills LLC property where hiking on the trails is permitted.
Follow the road across from Old Sandwich Club east up the hill. Pass the water
reservoir. Near the top, you will pass the road to the fire tower. If you detour to the

20

fire tower, on a nice day they might throw you down the key and let you come up for a grand view in all directions.

Not much past the fire tower access road there will be a trail to the left or north. It will go for almost a mile until you reach an interesting rotary (?) After looking around make a sharp left (~8 o'clock) and go southwest. Follow the **road/trail** downhill till you reach a cross road, Cathedral Road, and follow it south to the power lines and just beyond the power lines go half right or southwest at the trails intersection. This will take you back to the car.

Fire Tower and Manomet Hill Trail

e. **Cathedral Road to Ridge, Fire Tower and Ridge Overlook**

Directions and parking
Take Exit 3 from Hwy 3. Go east to Old Sandwich Road; turn left. This is a bumpy but wide dirt road for more than a mile. Go about two miles to the entrance of the Old Sandwich Club. Park across the street, on the east side of the road just north of the fire road. Be sure to leave access to the fire road open.
Approximate GPS street address: 248 Old Sandwich Rd, Plymouth, MA

Hike Difficulty
About 4 miles, 2 hrs, several hills.

Features

Cathedral Road; Manomet Hill; Fire Tower; Pinehills water Tank; Ridge Overlook; Sacrifice Rock.

Sacrifice Rock[4] is an historic Native American site in the Pine Hills region, in the northern section of *The Pinehills* residential project on Old Sandwich Road. The site is owned by the Plymouth Antiquarian Society. In 1928, Sacrifice Rock was gifted to the Antiquarian Society by Albert A. Raymond. In 1940, cement posts were erected to mark the site. A commemorative stone marker was added about 1960; this was replaced by a metal plaque in 1991.

The Hike

The whole hike is within Pine Hills LLC property, where hiking on the trails is permitted.

The trail, Cathedral Drive or Road, starts just to the left of the fire road and goes diagonally NE away from the fire road. After about ¼ mile, make a sharp right and follow the trail around until it goes NE again. At the power lines, go straight across. After 1/3 of a mile there is a trail going up the hill to the left. It is a climb, but the view is great. Return to the trail. Continue and stay to your right. Eventually you get to a straight, narrow dirt road. Turn south. When you emerge by the power lines go right and then left to the Fire Tower. Sometimes it is possible to be invited up the Fire tower when it is occupied. At the fire tower go around it to the right to the south side. From there bushwhack south to the power lines, about 100 feet. Just across the power line clearing and west of the power line pole a narrow trail goes south. A steep downhill followed by an uphill. (Surprise!) When you emerge on another trail, you can go about ¼ miles to the left for a view of Manomet and White Horse Beach. There turn around and follow the dirt road trail down to Sacrifice Rock Road. Go by Seaton Highlands and on to Old Sandwich Road. There, just north of Sacrifice Rock Road, on the right a Pinehills nature trail starts that will take you back to the parking area.

Cathedral Road   View North

22

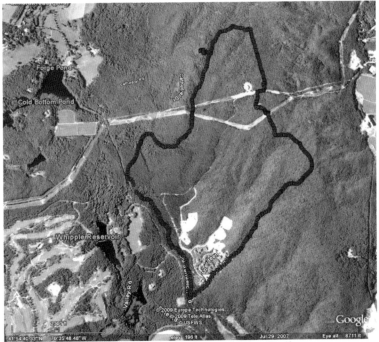

Manomet Hill, Fire Tower, Ridge Trail

2.   From Seaton Highlands:

a) Ridge Overlook down to Manomet up to Fire Tower and back

Directions
Take Exit 3 from Hwy 3. Go east on Clark Road. Turn left into The Pinehills. Turn onto Stonebridge Road. Follow it to the end. Turn left Old Sandwich Road. Turn right into Sacrifice Rock Road and then turn left into Seton Highlands and park in the Clubhouse parking lot. Approximate GPS address: 2 Seaton Highland, Plymouth,

Features
Ridge Overlook with a bay view; quiet wood trails; bogs.

Hike
From the parking lot go back to Sacrifice Rock Road and follow it up hill. At the boulder barrier, cross over and follow the dirt road all the way to the Ridge Overlook where it dead-ends. Great view to the east here. Now take the trail going downhill and east. It exits the area about 3 o'clock from where you entered. Follow it downhill till you are almost down to the bog. Now turn left, follow the power lines north, and take the first trail to the left. Follow it uphill and to the ridge of Manomet Hill. Turn left and follow the almost straight trail to the power lines by the Fire Tower. After

23

admiring the view of Cape Cod Bay turn left onto the fire tower road. Go around the tower to the right. From the southern corner of the tower enclosure bushwhack about 100 yards over to another set of power lines. Once you emerge by the power lines look for a small trail heading south. Follow it downhill. Stay left and make your way back uphill and emerge on what turns into Sacrifice Rock Road. Turn right and make your way back to Seaton Highlands.

Ridge Overlook down and up East slope Fire Tower and back

b. Across Manomet Hill, South Ridge and back

Directions
Take Exit 3 from Hwy 3. Go east on Clark Road. Turn left into The Pinehills. Turn onto Stonebridge Road. Follow it to the end. Turn left Old Sandwich Road. Turn right into Sacrifice Rock Road and then turn left into Seton Highlands and park in the Clubhouse parking lot.
Approximate GPS address: 2 Seaton Highland, Plymouth, MA

Features
Ridge Overlook with a bay view; quiet wood trails; bogs along Beaver Dam Road.

Difficulty
3.3 miles 1 ½ hours. Some steep up and downs.

Hike
From the parking lot go back to Sacrifice Rock Road and follow it up hill. At the boulder barrier, cross over and follow the dirt road all the way to the Ridge Overlook where it dead-ends. Great view to the east here. Now take the trail going downhill and east. It exits the area about 3 o'clock from where you entered. Follow it downhill, stay left till you get to the bog and then turn right and follow the perimeter of the bog to its south-southwest corner. Turn southwest and follow the trail along the power line. It will be on your left. Pass up the first trail east or to your right. Once you see houses and a coulter sac on your left there will be another trail to your right. Don't go northwest or a sharp right. Take the one that takes you southwest or half right and away from the from the power line. Follow it uphill till it emerges on the dirt road you had been on earlier. Turn left and head back down to Sacrifice Rock Road and Seton Highlands.

Bog off Beaver Dam Road   Glacial Erratic

Over The Ridge Trail

c.   South Ridge

Directions and parking
Take Exit 3 from Hwy 3. Go east to Old Sandwich Road; turn left. This is a bumpy but wide dirt road for more than a mile. Park on Old Tavern Trail (left) or Long Ridge Rd (right).
Approximate GPS street address: 523 Old Sandwich Rd, Plymouth, MA

Hike Difficulty
About 3.5 miles; 1:25 hrs, some gentle ups, and some steep ups and downs in the woods.

Features:
This hike is along the ridge that will eventually become Long Ridge Rd. Therefore, it may not be available in a 2 or 3 years. There are several opportunities to look east to Cape Cod Bay. Stone Soup Tavern; Sacrifice Rock.

The Hike
The whole hike is on Pine Hills LLC property, where hiking on the trails is permitted. Start on the trail just west of the Stone Soup Tavern driveway. Go north. After crossing the golf path, stay to your right. About 100 feet before you emerge on the golf course there is a trail to the right. When you get to Stonebridge Road, cross,

and continue the trail a little to the right. When the trail emerges across from Sacrifice Rock, cross over and follow Sacrifice Rock Road up hill. At the boulder barrier, cross over and follow the dirt road all the way to the Ridge Overlook where it dead-ends. Great view to the east here. Turn around and go back about ¼ miles. The road will turn right. Look for 4-foot wide trail. There should be orange plastic strips on the trees a little bit in. This 4-foot path winds and twists south for about a mile. Near the end, there will be two steep ups and downs with houses visible on the right. At the bottom of the steep down turn right or west and make your way out to Long Ridge Road. Follow it about ½ miles to the right and to the parked cars.

Cape Cod Bay from the Ridge

Another Glacial Erratic

South Ridge Trail

27

3. From Long Ridge Road:
a.   Over South Ridge/Manomet Valley/ Back
Directions
From Rt. 3 Exit 3 head east on Clark Road. After ~ a mile make a left onto Long Ridge Road. Go past Wickertree. Park on the road in Sedgewood on the left or Hickorywood on the right.
Approximate GPS address 99 Long Ridge Road

Features
Steep up and downs; pines, sand pits; views of Manomet.

Difficult
Only 2.1 miles or 1.5 miles. Steep tough rutted trails.

Hike
From Hickorywood or Sedgewood walk south to where Long Ridge makes a sharp left and right. Here you turn left into the woods and head up hill till you see a trail to your right again heading uphill. At the top of the hill there will be a trail to the left or east and then heading down hill. Near the bottom of the hill turn left and go almost north in the direction of the power lines. After about 1/3 of a mile there is a short cut to the left. Staying on the trail and not taking the short cut you will get to the sand pits. Stay to the left and follow the left perimeter of the pits. Near the northern end there are over grown areas. Continue north and onto a trail going past the sand and passing water on the right. After less than a ¼ mile there is a trail heading sharp left up the hill approximately south west. Follow that uphill till you meet the trail that runs along the ridge. Turn left or south. Follow that trail south for almost a mile till there are two steep up hills and too steep down hills, and the houses of Hickorywood can be seen through the trees. At the bottom of the steep hill turn right and follow the gentler slope down to Long Ridge Road.

A little color in the Pine Hills

Across South Ridge Trail

B.   The Pinehills

The Pinehills is a large, mostly residential development located in the Pine Hills region of Plymouth, Massachusetts. As of 2008, the project is the largest new residential and commercial development in New England.[1] The community consists of over 1,000 luxury houses, apartments and condominiums, three golf courses, a country club, and the Village Green, a small commercial center with shops and services. It is still under construction. When completed in 2014, it is expected to contain close to 3,000 homes and stretch over an area of 3,060 acres (12.4 km^2), an area larger than many Massachusetts towns. The houses in The Pinehills are broken into several small neighborhoods.[4]

Little Red Barn at The Pinehills Entrance

Hikes in The Pinehills

1.   Around Old Sandwich Club

Directions and Parking
Take Exit 3 from Hwy 3. Go east on Clark Road. Turn left into The Pinehills. Turn onto Stonebridge Road. Follow it to almost to the end. Turn left into Double Brook and park along the road.
Approximate GPS address: 99 Double Brook Rd, Plymouth, MA

Hike Difficulty
4.3 miles, 1:45 hrs, one gradual long uphill, rest is flat or downhill.

Features
An abandoned cranberry bog, ponds, pines, perimeter of Old Sandwich Club, four old stone bridges, and Sacrifice Rock[4]
Sacrifice Rock is an historic Native American site in the Pine Hills region, in the northern section of *The Pinehills* residential project on Old Sandwich Road. The site is owned by the Plymouth Antiquarian Society. In 1928, Sacrifice Rock was gifted to the Antiquarian Society by Albert A. Raymond. In 1940, cement posts were erected to mark the site. A commemorative stone marker was added about 1960; a metal plaque replaced this in 1991.
Old Sandwich Club: http://www.osgolfclub.com/Club/Scripts/Home/home.asp
The whole hike is on Pine Hills LLC property, where hiking on the trails is allowed.

The Hike
Follow Double Brook Road to the gravel road on the left, just short of the gatehouse. Now follow the gravel/dirt road staying to the right. You will pass by a pond on the right. Stay right and then go between a bog and the pond. Turn left/west along the bog and follow Valley Road up the hill partly along the fence of Old Sandwich Club. When you get to a 'T' in the road at the top of the hill turn right/north and cross over the rocks blocking the road. Follow this trail until you are blocked by a gate/fence. At that point, you need to go off trail for about 50 feet to your left/west. There will be another dirt trail going north. Follow it almost all the way to the power lines. Before you get to the power lines, just as the fence of the Old Sandwich Club starts turning east, turn right to the fence and follow the fence downhill until you get to a fire hydrant in the middle of the path. From there take the road downhill until you get to a 'T'. Turn left/north. To the south is the private Old Sandwich Club. Follow the dirt road north over 3-4 stone bridges. At the end of the road cross Old Sandwich Road and enter the woods just south of where you emerged. Follow that trail to Cathedral Road, turn right, and follow it out to Old Sandwich Road. Make a sharp left, onto the fire road. Just past the gate, make a right onto the Pinehills Trail going

south. At Sacrifice Rock cross the road and continue on the trail until you can see the gatehouse. Parked cars are now just south of the gatehouse.

The Pinehills Bog

Old Stonebridge

Sacrifice Rock

Around Old Sandwich Club Trail

2.   The Pinehills Bog and Pond
Directions and parking
Take Exit 3 from Hwy 3. Go east on Clark Road. Turn left into The Pinehills. Follow the road, and then turn onto Stonebridge Road. Follow it to almost the end. Turn left into Double Brook and park.
Mapping address: 99 Double Brook Rd, Plymouth, MA

Difficulty
Short hike; 1:10 hrs, about two miles; flat.

Features
Old stone bridges, pines, ponds and a bog; Whipple Reservoir, Former Talcott Estate; Old Sandwich Club.

The Hike
After parking on Double Brook walk on the left and take the gravel road on the left. Follow it staying to the right. You will pass a pond on the right and a bog on the left. Turn right after the bog. Just before the stone bridge, there is a trail to the left. It will take you north along the west edge of Whipple Reservoir across from the Talcott residence. At the end of the trail, you can see Whipple Reservoir dam, and one of the Old Sandwich Golf Club holes. Turn around; beyond here, you are definitely on private property even though there are no signs. When you get back, just past the bridge on the left is a quaint old green gate. The trail behind it is somewhat more obscure, but does lead to another view of the pond. Again, turn around at the pond. When you come back to the dirt road, also just past the bridge, there is a little trail to the right leading to a water gate and a great view of the pond to the south. Return to the dirt road and follow it staying to the right. Make a right when you come to the T.

Follow the dirt road. Just past the pond, there are tracks from a former dirt road. It is fairly overgrown but does give you a chance to proceed further along the pond if you want to get another view or just explore. At some point, the vegetation will get too thick to proceed. Return and follow the dirt road until you can see the gatehouse. There will be green electric boxes on the right. Cross over to the original gravel road here to avoid the gate on the way back to your car.

Pinehills Bog

Old Stone Bridge

Forge Pond Bridge

Talcott Residence

Bog and Pond trail

3. The Pinehills-South

Directions and parking
From Rt. 3 Exit 3 take Clark Road to the Pinehills. Turn right into The Pinehills by the Red Barn. Park in the parking lot behind the shops and post office. Approximate GPS street address: Neighborhood Green N, Plymouth, MA

Hike Difficulty
About 5 miles; 2:10 hrs, some hills; all on paved or wood trails or dirt road

Features:
Neighborhoods of The Pinehills. The whole hike is on Pine Hills LLC property, where hiking on the trails is permitted.

The Hike
Pick up the paved trail at the north corner of the parking lot and head north. Follow the paved trail being careful to stay on the walking trail along Stonebridge Road and do not get diverted to a golf cart trail. When you get to Old Tavern Trail, cross over, and follow the trail on the right down Old Tavern Trail. Cross over Old Sandwich

Road and follow Long Ridge Road to where it ends on Clark Road across from Great Island. Cross over to the Great Island side and find the trail heading west along Clark Road. Follow the trail alongside Clark Road and cross back over when it does. Follow it west crossing five cross roads. Continue west when you see the fire station on your right. You will come to a coulter sac and an old dirt road heading north. Follow it to the Avalon Apartments. Climb down the hill to the road and then follow the road north of the new apartments and make your way back to the Village Square.

Forgotten Sign

Typical walk   Boulder along the way

The Pinehills South
4.   **West Pinehills, Bog, Winslow's View**

36

Directions and parking
Off Rt3 take Exit 3 and follow signs to The Pinehills. Enter The Pinehills and go to Stonebridge Road. Follow Stonebridge Road about 1 mile and turn left into Winslow's View. Go about another 0.5 miles and turn left to park behind the Winslow's View Village Center by the tennis courts.
Approximate GPS street address: 10 Peter Brown Cartway, Plymouth, MA

Hike Difficulty
About 3.2 miles, 1:05 hrs, one long uphill, a few short ups and downs.

Features
Winslow's View, The Pinehills bog and pond, old Valley Road, and glimpses of Old Sandwich Golf Club.

The Hike
The whole hike is on Pine Hills LLC property, where hiking on the trails is permitted. On foot take the path on the north corner of the tennis court parking lot and work your way back out to Stonebridge Road, either through the neighborhoods or on the main road. Once on Stonebridge Road turn left and take the footpath on the left.

South of Old Sandwich Club   The Pinehills Bog

Follow it all the way to the bottom of the hill and turn left onto Doublebrook. Follow Doublebrook until, just before the gatehouse, you can turn left onto a dirt road (formerly Crest Ridge Road). Follow it staying right until you reach the passage between the pond and bog. At that point, turn left along the edge of the bog and head up hill on 'Valley Road'. The dirt road will pass Old Sandwich Golf Club on the right before it gets to a T. Turn left or south and follow former Sanderson Road till you see The Pinehills Jones Course, straight ahead. Turn left towards Winslow's View. When you reach the houses go left and pass between the two fences or go right and up to the small parking area at end of Benjamin's Gate. The road will return you to the Winslow's View village center.

West Pinehills Trail

C.   Further South off Old Sandwich

Distribution of Hikes

38

1.   Four Ponds Hike (Manomet)
2.   Hathaway Pond
3.   Morey Hole, Briggs Reservoir
4.   Talcott Plot

1.   Four Ponds Hike: Great Island Pond, Little Island Pond, Beaver Dam Pond, and Shallow Pond (Manomet)

Directions
Take exit 3 east from Hwy 3 onto Clark Road. Go just past the Town Transfer Station and either park on the road near the sign indicating the Town Conservation area, or use the dirt road to turn into the town Conservation area.
Approximate GPS street address: 372 Beaver Dam Rd, Plymouth, MA

Hike Difficulty
About 4.5 miles, 1:30 hrs, flat except for a couple of small hills.

Features:
Little Island Pond; Great Island Pond; Shallow Pond; Beaver Dam Pond. Pines, ponds, and bogs.
Great Island Pond[4] , known officially as Island Pond, is a 49-acre pond , one of three ponds known as *Island Pond* within the town (One is located near South Pond village, and the other is located in the Cedarville section of town). The pond is located in the eastern portion of *The Pinehills* development south of Little Island Pond.
Long Island Pond[4], also known as Little Island Pond, is a 30-acre pond located in the eastern portion of *The Pinehills* development north of Great Island Pond and south of Beaver Dam Pond.
Beaver Dam Pond[4] is a 30-acre pond in the Manomet section and is located north of Little Island Pond, west of Fresh Pond, and east of the Pine Hills. The pond is the headwaters of Beaver Dam Brook. The water quality is impaired due to non-native plants.
Shallow Pond[4] is an 18-acre pond in the Manomet section, south of Fresh Pond, north of Briggs Reservoir, southwest of Cedar Bushes and west of Manomet Beach. The water quality is impaired due to non-native aquatic plants and nuisance exotic species.
The hike starts on Town of Plymouth Conservation Land. The land by Shallow Pond is owned by Indian Brook Cranberry Bogs Co.

Great Island Pond

The Hike

After entering the Town Conservation Area proceed to the edge of Little Island Pond and proceed around the pond to the right. After you pass the pond stay on the trail going southeast. Cross the dirt road a little to your left and go over the small hill down to the water of Great Island Pond. From the beach, proceed to the left by going up a sandy patch to a dirt road. Follow the dirt road to the right to the southwest tip of Great Island Pond for another view. Continue on the dirt road. Stay to the left of the bogs and before the last bog; make a left to Shallow Pond.

Now retrace your steps to the southwest tip of Great Island Pond and take a trail to the right due north. When you get to the crossroad, stay right, go past the houses, and then turn left to Beaver Dam Pond. In the spring, there is a growth of water marigolds right where the trail meets the water. From Beaver Dam Pond return and stay to the right. This leads to Hollis Road. Past the houses follow the pond around to the left and return to the Town Conservation Area and the car.

40

Four Pond Hike Map
2.   Hathaway Pond

Directions and Parking
From Rt.3 Exit 3 go east on Clark Rd. Go about ½ mile and turn right onto Old Sandwich Rd. Go about 2.7 miles. You will pass Sip Pond Rd on the right at first and then on the left. Keep going till you get to a dirt road on the right with two openings.Turn right and cross the next dirt road.. Then stay left at the fork and this bumpy dirt road will take you to Dugaway Pond and an open area for parking. If you are in a standard car and don't have a lot of clearance you might want to park by the first crossing and hike the ¼ mile to Dugaway Pond.
Approximate GPS address: 1235 Old Sandwich Road, Plymouth, MA 02360

Features
Ponds, bogs, and pine forest. Dugaway Pond, Hathaway Pond., Ellis Bog, and Valinor Farm (www.valinorfarm.com)
Valinor Farm, located on 45 acres, offers a variety of riding disciplines with focus on eventing.
Since part of the hike is along Valinor Farm land you may want to give them a call (508 224-3332) to see whether it is ok to walk along the edge of their property on a particular day. The rest of the hike is also on private property, but there are no "No Trespassing" signs along the way at this time.

Difficulty
2.8 miles, about 1:20 hr, some short steep hills.

Hike
After you step out of your car by Dunaway Pond, Ellis Bog will be to your lft or south. The trail starts between the pond and the bog going west southwest. Follow the trail to the first interesection, less than ¼ mile. Stay left and follow the trail all the way to the power lines and Rt 3. Turn right and follow the powerlines north. The sandy tracks will turn down hill and you will notice Hathaway Pond on the right. Stay left and there will be a trail between Hathaway Pond and a highway fence. Now go up the hill ans stay right. Past the top of the hill there will be a trail into the forest on your right. Follow the trail for ~1/4 mile. Turn north not east. When you come to a gate stay to the right of the gate and turn right. You are now on a riding trail. At the bottom of the hill turn left and go uphill. Now you will pass a large grassy area, all part of Valinor Farm. Stay to your right and then go down the hill. You will come to

Valinor Farm

An open area with water on the right, a hill in the middle, and a dirt road on the left. Take the trail up the hill, pass the house on the left and staying to your right, follow along the farm fences till you can go no further. Now make a right into the woods and bushwack east about 500 feet and down to a dirt road and bog. Turn right and follow around the bog staying right. Just short of the south end of the bogs turn right and go over the little hill. When you meet another trail turn left and follow the trail which will take you back to Dugaway Pond and your car.

Dugaway Pond   **Icy Hathaway Pond**

Hathaway Pond Trail

42

3.   Morey Hole-Briggs Reservoir

Directions
From Rt-3 Exit 3 take Clark Rd east. Turn right on Old Sandwich Rd; go 1.7 mi.
You will see a dirt road with a gate on the left. Pass that up. Park by the second or
southern gate, just before where Ship Pond Rd comes in on the right.
Approximate GPS address 1004 Old Sandwich Rd., Plymouth, MA

Features
Morey Hole, Briggs Reservoir; bogs; pines
Morey Hole[4] (also known as Morey's Hole), is a 22-acre (89,000 m^2) pond, west of
Vallerville and Ship Pond, and southwest of Briggs Reservoir. Camp Child, a former
summer camp run by the Old Colony Council of the Boy Scouts of America from
1925 through 1995, surrounds the pond.
Briggs Reservoir[4] is a 28-acre (110,000 m^2) reservoir located in the Manomet section
of town south of Shallow Pond, southwest of Manomet Beach, northwest of
Vallerville and northeast of Morey Hole. Indian Brook flows through the reservoir.
There are two unnamed islands in the reservoir.
Most of the land, except for the bogs, around both bodies of water is now owned by
the Town of Plymouth

Difficulty
4.2 miles, 1 ½ hrs, some short hills.

Hike
After parking by the gate go around the gate and stay to your right. The land to the
right is owned by the Town of Plymouth, that to the left by Briggs Bogs. Walk over
to the bog and follow the dirt road to the right of the bog. After about ¼ miles take
the dirt road to the left which leads to Indian Brook Road. At Indian Brook Rd take a
right, and then go straight. Briggs Reservoir is now on your right. Continue over ½
mile along the reservoir till you see a house on the left. Here, although not marked
Indian Brook Rd leaves the town property and turns private. Go about 100 ft on the
private road and then turn sharp right, go past the gate and walk southeast by the
northern end of Briggs Reservoir. You are now back on town property. Go straight
till you get to another gate. Turn left just before the gate. Following that trail, you
will see another large bog area on your left, followed by a wooded area on your left.
Continue straight past the wooded area. When you come to the T just past the bog on
your right, turn right, and then stay left and you will get to yet another gate, beyond
which is Savery Road. Turn right and follow Savery Road less than a 1/4 mile. Then
find and take the trail to the left. After about 200 feet you will see houses. Turn right.
Just past the houses, bear left going towards Morey Hole and then turn right and
follow the trail essentially straight till after you pass some deteriorating structures on
the right. At the next junction, go right. Going left will take you to a view of Morey
Hole. After the right turn go sharp left at the next junction. This will take you down
to a dam between Morey Hole and Briggs Reservoir. Turn left here and then go

straight for about ¼ mile. Look for a trail off to the right. You can just see the clearing for the bogs in the distance from the junction. Turn right and follow the trail till you emerge on the bog where you started out. The car will be behind the gate to the left.

Briggs Reservoir

Morey Hole

Split Rock with color

Bog Barn

Morey Hole-Briggs Reservoir Trail Map

44

4.   Talcott Parcel

Directions
Off Rt. 3 take Clark Road east. Make right at Old Sandwich Road. Go about one mile. Park just beyond or under the power lines on the left.
Approximate GPS street address: 862 Old Sandwich Rd, Plymouth, MA

Hike Difficulty
The hike is 3.7 miles, 1:40 hrs., Only minor hills, except for one very steep downhill about 2/3 of the way.

Features:
Large wooded parcel owned by Town of Plymouth, Wildlands Trust and some private owners. Reid Pond, Cotton Pond; No special features, just a nice walk in the woods.

The Hike
Start the hike on the trail going west just north of the power lines. It will take you around a small pond and under the power lines. Now just follow the trail southwest without going out on the power line trail. After ~ 3/4 of a mile, the trail will turn sharply south and will go parallel to Rt.3. After another ¾ mile, it will turn and meander east. Go down the very steep decline and at the bottom turn right and bushwhack southeast for ~100 -200 feet till you get to a trail. Follow the trail north and then east for ~1/4 mile. Before it turns left and downhill, stop and turn right to make your way out to Ship Pond Road southeast. Follow Ship Pond Road northeast for about ¼ mile to the entrance of Emery Preserve East (Wildlands Trust) on the left. Follow the marked trail northeast through an open pine area. The trail continues in the northeast corner on to Cotton Pond . Just before the pond on the right take a left that takes you out to Old Sandwich Road. Once on Old Sandwich Road turn left and walk back to the parking area by the power lines.

Cotton Pond

45

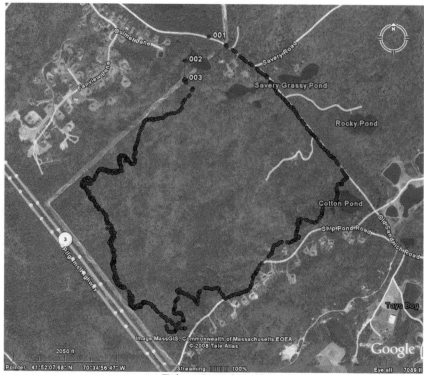

Talcott Parcel Trail

III.   The Ponds off Long Pond Road

Hikes from North to South
1.   Russell Mill Pond
2.   Hoyts Pond
3.   Boot Pond
4.   PSHS to Clark Rd
5.   Six Ponds Conservation Area
6.   Halfway Pond Area
7.   Gramp's Loop
8.   Around Halfway Pond
9.   Bloody Pond
10.   Agawam to Fawn Pond
11.   Makepeace Bogs
12.   White Island Bogs
13.   Hedges Pond
14.   Pickerel Pond

Distribution of Hikes off Long Pond

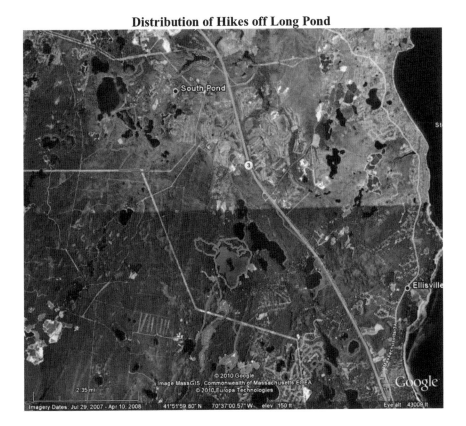

1. Russell Mill Pond

Directions
From Rt.3, take exit 5. Turn left and follow Long Pond Road about one ½ miles to
Boot Pond Road. The Nature Conservancy office is just south, across the street, on
the left, at 190 Long Pond Road. Follow their driveway until you can find a parking
spot that does not block their access. You may want to stop at the office to let them
know where you have parked and that you will be hiking in the area.
Approximate GPS address: 204 Long Pond Rd, Plymouth, MA

Features
Russell Mill Pond, Russell Mill Remnants, Gilbert Trout Hatchery, beautiful pond,
quiet woods.
Russell Millpond[4], also known as Russell Mill Pond, is a 42-acre pond in
Chiltonville village. Fed by springs and water from cranberry bogs, the outflow of
the pond is the Eel River.

47

The Gilbert Trout Hatchery, since its foundation in 1869, has been dedicated to raising and selling trout (brook and rainbow). Some customers have been as far away as Canada while most are a bit closer to the hatchery's location in Chiltonville, a hamlet in southern Plymouth. Much of this pristine land is devoted to the raising of trout as it has been for 139 years. Contact page: http://gilberttrout.com/index.html
The Eel River is a 3.9-mile river mostly in the village of Chiltonville in Plymouth. Its headwaters are springs and small ponds above Russell Millpond. Its watershed encompasses approximately 15 square miles. It flows along Plimoth Plantation and Plymouth Beach for about ½ mile before emptying into Plymouth Harbor between the beach and Manters Point.

Difficulty
3.9 miles, 1:55 hrs, some hills, some less used trails.

Hike
The first part of the hike will all be on Town of Plymouth land. Park and then walk to the right of the Nature Conservancy office. You will soon reach the point where the Eel River flows into Russell Mill Pond. Cross the bridge and stay to the right. Follow the trail/road until you reach the road, King Fisher Lane. Follow it staying to the left out to Jordan Road. Follow Jordan Road to the left until you can turn left onto Russell Mills Road. Look for the dam where Eel River overflows going east. Follow the road till it turns sharply to the right/north. Here look for a driveway on the left that will take you to an access to a power line clearing. Stay to the right. When you reach the power lines, turn right. You are now on RUSSELL MILLS ROAD REALTY TRUST property. The trail is overgrown and not obvious, but it is there along the right. Follow the power lines southwest to a clearing, almost 1/2 mile. You are entering the Gilbert Trout Hatchery. The owner had no objection to us hiking across and around the pond. Now turn left and find the narrow bridge across the brook. If you run into fish retainers, you have gone too far. Once across follow the narrow trail to a wider trail, formerly East Russell Mills Road. It will lead to the pond. Turn around and follow a trail to the left or west. Follow that trail till you get to what appears to be a day camp on VEGA SOCIAL CLUB INC property. Stay to you right and take the road past the gate up to an open area and power lines. You are now on NStar and Town of Plymouth land. Cross the power line area and look for a trail on your left going back down to the pond and the bridge. At the bridge turn right and make your way back to the Nature Conservancy office and your car.

Russell Mill Pond

48

2009   Inflow   2010

2008   Outflow   2011

Russell Mill Pond Hike

49

2.   Hoyts Pond

Directions
From Rt.3, take exit 5. Turn left and follow Long Pond Road about 1 ½ miles to the small parking lot with split rail fencing on the right, right after Boot Pond Road. It is across the street from the well-hidden Nature Conservancy office.
Approximate GPS address: 181 Long Pond Rd, Plymouth, MA

Features
Eel River Conservation Area bogs historically known as Jenkins Hole, Hoyts Pond, Gunners Exchange Pond, glimpses of Negro Pond and Turtle Pond, quiet calm woods and bogs.
Hoyts Pond is at latitude and longitude coordinates 41.8957 and -70.6523 and the altitude is 82 feet (25 meters).
Gunners Exchange Pond[4] is a 29-acre pond in the southern part of South Pond village within the Eel River watershed, southeast of Boot Pond, southwest of Island Pond, and northeast of Myles Standish State Forest. The outflow is Hoyts Pond, which is connected to Gunners Exchange Pond.

Difficulty
2.7 (1:15 hrs) or 5.3 miles (2:20) depending on if you just walk to Hoyts Pond or if you continue around Hoyts Pond and Gunners Exchange Pond. No hills on the walk to Hoyts Pond. Some short hills on the east side of Hoyts Pond and Gunners Exchange.

Hike
2.7-miles hike.
Park and find the trail in the right/northwest corner near Boot Pond Road. Follow the trail marked by Wildlands Trust to the bog area. Once you emerge by the bogs turn right and head south. You will pass by five bogs in the process of being returned to their pre-cranberry state. As you, pass the last bog look for a trail south into the woods. It will take you to Hoyts Pond. Once at Hoyts pond you can turn around, return to the bogs, and then follow the path to the right along the south side of the bogs for variety. As you approach Long Pond Road, you will have to work your way back to the car along the road.

Pump in the bog

Eel River bog prior to naturalization

5.3-mile hike
Park and find the trail in the right/southwest corner near Boot Pond Road. Follow the trail marked by Wildlands Trust to the bog area. Once you emerge by the bogs turn right and head south. You will pass by five bogs in the process of being returned to their pre-cranberry state. As you pass the last bog, look for a trail south into the woods. It will take you to Hoyts Pond. At Hoyts Pond note the road (Ben Raymond Rd.) on the right and take it up to College Pond Road. Turn left and follow College Pond Road till after you pass Turtle and Negro Ponds on the right after ~ ½ mile and Gunnery Exchange Pond on the left. After about one mile overall on College Pond Road take the dirt road on the left formerly known as Crooked Pond Road. After ~ ¼ mile, turn left or north on a dirt road (Gunnery Exchange Road). Follow it to the bog, less than ½ miles. At the bog, stay left and then go straight north into the woods when the road turns southwest. Follow that trail just above the shore of Hoyts Pond until it emerges on the trail back to the Eel River Conservation Area bogs. Turn right and return to the bogs. Then follow the path to the right along the bogs for variety. As you approach Long Pond Road, you will have to work your way back to the car along the road.

Hoyts Pond   Eel River springs

A little color in the pines

51

2.7 mile & 5.3 mile hike

3.   Boot Pond

Directions and parking
From Rt.3 Exit 5 take Long Pond Road south to Boot Road on the right.
Or
From Rt.3 Exit 3 take Long Pond Road north to Boot Road on the left.
Follow Boot Road to Knotty Pines Lane. Park at the triangle at Knotty Pines, May
Hill Rd, and Boot Road intersection.
Approximate GPS address: 100 Boot Pond Road, Plymouth, MA

Hike Difficulty
2.5 miles; about 1 hour, some short hills. 4.7 miles; about 1:45 hrs, some short hills.

Features:
Boot Pond, Great South Pond, Negro Pond, Turtle Pond, Hallfield Pond; Old Bog
Road.
Boot Pond[4] is a 76-acre pond within the Eel River watershed. The pond is located
west of South Pond village, northwest of Gunners Exchange Pond and Hoyts Pond,
and north of Myles Standish State Forest. The pond is a secondary municipal water
supply for the Town of Plymouth.

Great South Pond[4] is a 292-acre (1.2 km^2) reservoir in South Pond village. The pond is within the Eel River watershed, located southeast of Little South Pond, west of South Triangle Pond, and north of Boot Pond. The pond serves as a secondary municipal water supply for the Town of Plymouth.

Red-Bellied Turtle

Bog Irrigation

The Hike
Boot Road turns into May Hill Road. After parking follow May Hill Road. Stay left. Boot Pond will appear on the left, Great South Pond on the right. As you head south from Boot Pond, you come to the junction of Old Bog Road and Hog Rock Road. If you continue around Boot Pond on Old Bog Road, you will do a 2.5-mile hike. If you continue on Hog Rock Road, you will do a 4.7-mile hike.

2.5-mile hike
Old Bog Road is a private dirt road. You use it at your own risk, and be aware that the owners have no responsibility if you choose to use it. Respect it and stay on the road. As the road runs out there will be a driveway on your left. Walk towards the house. Just before the house turn right and go up the slope. A trail starts in the middle of the slope in the west corner of the yard. Follow the narrow trail to an opening between Boot Pond and an abandoned bog. You are now on Town property. Stay right and follow the dirt road on the east side of the bog. Continue on the dirt road. It will pass between Negro Pond and Boot Pond. When you can see the paved road ahead make a sharp left unto another dirt road and you will be heading north on Knotty Pines Lane between Hallfield Pond and Boot Pond and it will take you back to Boot Pond Road and the car will be just to your left.
4.7-mile hike
Take Hog Rock Road continue on it for about 3/4 mile. There will be a blue marker on the left and an open area ahead. This is Myles Stadish State Forest. Look for the trail cutting back, going very sharp east or left within a few feet of the blue marker and in the open area. It is the only left since you have been on Hog Rock Road. Follow it till you get to the powerlines. Turn east or left and follow the power lines past the transformer station to Snake Hill Road.Turn left or north and follow Snake Hill Road for over 1 mile till you reach a junction with two dirt roads. Go straight onto the dirt road, up the slope, and continue north to Boot Pond Road. Turn left and the car will be up the road to your left.

Boot Pond Trails

Vernal Pond

4. Between Clark Road and PSHS

The Town of Plymouth owns this property and conservation efforts are in the hands of Wildlands Trust. At the time of writing Plymouth Rock Studios are planning to develop the area north of the Plymouth South High School and to put a road through this area.

Directions and parking
From Rt. 3 Exit 3 turn west towards Long Pond Road. Make a right onto Long Pond Road. Go about ½ miles till you get to a 'u'-shaped turn-in on the right and park there.
Approximate GPS address: 545 Long Pond Rd, Plymouth, MA

Hike Difficulty
About 2.8 miles, 1:40 hours, short steep hills;

Features:
Vernal pond; area between Clark Road and Plymouth South High School.
This is Town of Plymouth land, but may someday be crossed by a road to Plymouth Rock Studios from south to north.

A vernal pool is a seasonal body of standing water that typically forms in the spring from melting snow and other runoff, dries out completely in the hotter months of summer, and often refills in the autumn. Vernal pools range from broad, heavily vegetated lowland bodies to smaller, isolated upland bodies with little permanent vegetation. They are free of fish and provide important breeding habitat for many terrestrial or semi aquatic species such as frogs, salamanders, and turtles.

The American Heritage® Science Dictionary Copyright © 2005 by Houghton Mifflin Company. Published by Houghton Mifflin Company. All rights reserved.

Plymouth South High School, also known as Plymouth South, PSHS, or, informally, P. South, is a public high school located in Plymouth, Massachusetts. Its students are residents of the town of Plymouth. The school is one of two high schools in Plymouth, the other being Plymouth North High School. Plymouth South is located near the Long Pond neighborhood of Plymouth, west of Route 3 and *The Pinehills* development. The school has an enrollment of approximately 927 students [1] in grades 9-12. The mascot is a panther.

The Hike
Start at the middle of the 'U'. Go east a few steps then turn right. Follow the cycle-scarred trail south until you can see cars on Clark Road and the trail turns left. Shortly make another left and follow the trail north. Follow the trail for about a mile till it meets another trail going right. This will take you close to the highway fence. Follow it about 500 feet. Then you will see a depression to the west, which hides the vernal pond. The pond is visible from the trail in the winter but not in the summer. The trail down to the pond is not easy to find nor easy to follow. The best route takes

you past three large consecutively placed boulders situated along the trail on the way down. Some of this will feel like there is no trail. It is best to return the same way. Then continue to follow the trail north. It will make a turn west and bring you up to the high school paved area. Follow it to near the beginning of the drive out, and reenter the trail to the left just before the drive. It will lead to a trail heading south along Longpond Road and back to the parking area.

Sandy Trail   **Vernal Pond**

Trail between PSHS and Clark Road

56

5.   Six Ponds Conservation Area East

Directions and parking
From Rt. 3 take exit 3 west towards Long Pond Road. Park just past the west ramp along the road.
Approximate GPS address: 50 Clark Rd, Plymouth, MA

Hike Difficulty
3-miles; 1 hour, a few short steep hills

Features:
Boulders; small meadows; nice uncomplicated walk; some road noise.
http://www.sixponds.org/site/map.html
You start out on Pine Hills LLC property, and continue on WildlandsTrust property.

The Hike
Carefully cross the road. By the guardrail look for a trail a few feet down but essentially parallel to the road going east. It will take you to the beginning of the trail going south. Follow it all the way to Ship Road. By Ship Road turn around and head back.

Flora   Glacial Boulder

Six Pond Area Hike

Lady Slipper

6. Halfway Pond Conservation Area

Directions and parking
From Rt. 3 Exit 3 turn west. Make a left onto Long Pond Road and an immediate right onto the continuation of Clark Road. Follow downhill and go left on West Long Pond Road. Pass between Long Pond and Gallows Ponds and then stay right. Take the unmarked dirt road (Gallows Pond Road) that follows the pond. Go about ¼ miles southwest. There will be a small parking area on the left and the beginning of Joe Brown Trail.
Approximate GPS street address: 100 Gallows Pond Rd, Plymouth, MA

Hike Difficulty
Two miles; 1 hr., some small hills

Features:
Halfway Pond; Gallows Pond; Rock in Gallows Pond; Long Pond; quiet woods and ponds.
Gallows Pond[4] is a 43-acre kettlehole pond west of and adjacent to Long Pond, south of Little Long Pond, and northeast of Halfway Pond. Camp Wind-in-the-Pines Girl Scout Center is located along the shore of this pond.

Long Pond[4] is a 211-acre cold water, east of Myles Standish State Forest, Halfway Pond and Round Pond, west of Route 3 at Exit 3, and north of West Wind Shores. The pond has an average depth of 46 feet and a maximum depth of 100 feet. It is fed by groundwater and an inlet from Little Long Pond, and drains into Halfway Pond. A paved boat ramp provided by the Public Access Board with ample parking spaces is easily accessible from Route 3. Long Pond Village4 to the southwest of the pond includes Faunce Church.

The Hike
Off Gallows Pond Road take Joe Brown Trail and follow it to the end. You will see Long Pond across west Long Pond Road. Turn around and take your first left over to Blackmer Hill trail. Turn right at junction and then left to go on Big Point Trail. Along here you will see Half Way Pond. Turn right onto Blackmer Hill Trail and then left onto Whippoorwill Trail. After you cross Gallows Pond Road on this trail, you will get to Gallows Pond Trail. Turn right and follow it. After you cross a wide dirt road to nowhere, the trail goes down to a large rock in Gallows Pond. Continue back up to the road and walk east back to the car.

Gallows Pond   Halfway Pond

Gallows Pond Rock   Pond through the pines

Halfway Pond Conservation Area

7. Gramp's Loop

Directions and parking
There are two ways to get there.
Long way, but smooth ride: From Rt.3 Exit 3 go west towards Long Pond Road.
Make a right on Long Pond Road and go about two miles till you get to Mast Road
on your left. Turn onto Mast Road and follow it just past the power lines and the
entrance to the Girls Scout camp. There will be a Wildlands trust parking area on
your right.
Or
Shorter but bumpy: Form Rt. 3 Exit 3 turn west. Make a left onto Long Pond Road
and an immediate right onto the continuation of Clark Road. Follow downhill and go
left on West Long Pond Road. Pass between Long Pond and Gallows Ponds and then
stay right. Take the unmarked dirt road (Gallows Pond Road) that follows the pond.
At Mast Road turn right and there will be a parking area about 100feet north.
Approximate GPS street address 500 Mast Rd, Plymouth, MA

Hike Difficulty:
Two miles, 55 minutes, small hills

Features:

Halfway Pond; grand stand of pines, quiet walk in the woods. The hike is all on Wildlands Trust Property.

The Hike

The trail starts from the southwest corner of the parking lot. Go almost south a short ways, till you reach a trail junction, and go right. Now follow the loop trail. At one point, there will be an intersection. Stay left and follow the 'Loop" trail till you return to the first intersection and head back down towards the parking area.

Gramp's Loop Trail

8.   Around Halfway Pond

Directions
From Hwy 3 Exit 3 turn west and take Longpond Road north. Alternatively, from Hwy3 Exit 5 turn west and take Longpond Road south. Turn west onto Mast Road; follow for ~ 2 miles till you see a Wildlands Trust parking area on the right. Approximate GPS street address: 500 Mast Rd, Plymouth, MA

Hike Difficulty
3.2 miles; 1:30 hrs, minor hills, mostly flat.

Features
Halfway Pond; cranberry bogs; water ducts; Round Pond; Long Pond; wood trails
Halfway Pond[4] is a 232-acre warm water pond located between Myles Standish State Forest and Long Pond, west of Round Pond, southwest of Gallows Pond, and north of Fawn Pond and White Island Pond. The average depth is nine feet and the maximum depth is 13 feet. The pond is fed by the outflow of Long Pond and drains into the Agawam River. Halfway Pond Island lies in the middle of the pond and is managed as a research natural area by The Nature Conservancy in Massachusetts. There are almost three miles of shoreline.
Long Pond[4] is a 211-acre cold water pond east of Myles Standish State Forest, Halfway Pond and Round Pond, west of Route 3 at Exit 3, and north of West Wind Shores. The pond has an average depth of 46 feet and a maximum depth of 100 feet. It is fed by groundwater and an inlet from Little Long Pond, and drains into Halfway Pond. A paved boat ramp provided by the Public Access Board with ample parking spaces is easily accessible from Route 3.
Gallows Pond[4] is a 43-acre kettlehole pond west of and adjacent to Long Pond, south of Little Long Pond, and northeast of Halfway Pond. Camp Wind-in-the-Pines Girl Scout Center is located along the shore of this pond. Long Pond Village to the southwest of the pond includes Faunce Church.

    Halfway Pond   **Long Pond**

The Hike
The hike is 3+ miles, all the way around Halfway Pond. Walk south from the parking lot and follow Mast Road around the pond to the right. After you pass Agawam Road on your left and just before you get to Halfway Pond Road, there is a turn into the woods on the left. This is Agawam Development LLC land. Respect their property

and stay on the dirt roads and trails. A large piece of concrete marks the beginning of the trail. Follow the trail to the left along the pond. After the bogs, follow the water flu till you can turn right or northeast. Follow that trail to the paved road. Turn left. Right after the house on the left take the trail into the WLT area. Follow the trail to Whippoorwill Trail, turn right and follow it all the way across Gallows Pond Road and then to Gallows Pond Trail. Turn left or west. This will bring you out on Mast Road just south of the parking area.

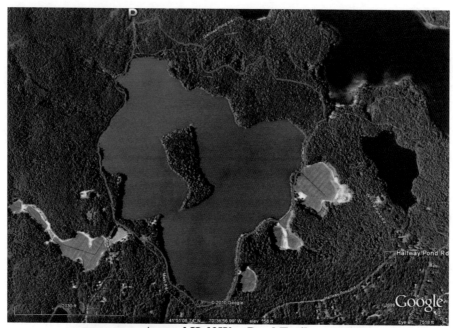

Around Half Way Pond Trail

64

9.   Bloody Pond

Directions to Bloody Pond Access:
If coming from north on Rt. 3 take exit 3. Turn left. Make a left onto Long Pond
Road. Go about 2.5 miles south. There will be a dirt road on the left. If coming from
the south take exit 2. Turn right on Long Pond Road. Go about 2.5 Miles. There will
be a dirt road on the right. Follow the dirt road to the gate. The trail starts just to the
right of the gate.
GPS street address 855 Long Pond Road, Plymouth, MA

Hike Difficulty
3.2 miles, 1:45 hrs, some hills; some bushwhacking

Features
Pines; Camp Baird, Bloody Pond
Bloody Pond[4] is a 98-acre (400,000 m^2) natural kettlehole pond near Long Pond
village. This pond, visible from the southbound side of Route 3 past the Ship Pond
Road bridge, is fed by groundwater and has over two miles (3 km) of shoreline. The
average depth is 17 feet (5.2 m) and the maximum depth is 38 feet (12 m). Legal
public access to the pond is obtained through a dirt road off Long Pond Road and is
suitable primarily for shore and wading anglers as the access point is a long walk
from a two-car parking lot in front of a gate.
Camp Baird is owned by Home for Little Wanderers.

The Hike:
The initial portion of the hike is on land owned by the Town of Plymouth
Start to right of gate across access road. Follow trail for about   1/2 mile. When you
get to the road, turn east. At the first major junction if you go left it will take you
down to the pond. Once at the pond you will have to turn back.

Bloody Pond -north   **Bloody Pond – south**

The trail bears to the right. Go left at the junction. After that, stay left to go north.
Follow the trail until you see the beach near the end. Just before you think, you will
soon be at the beach there is a small trail to the left, which actually takes you down
to the beach. The beach and north of it belongs to Camp Baird and is private
property. You will now have to turn around and return the way you came.

Bloody Pond Trail

10.   Agawam Road to Fawn Pond (North to south)

Directions
Off Rt3 Exit 3 start on CLARK RD (at RT-3 & CLARK RD in PLYMOUTH) going toward LONG POND RD - go 0.3 mi. Turn Left on LONG POND RD - go 1.6 mi. Turn Right on HALFWAY POND RD - go 1.6 mi. Turn Right on MAST RD - go 0.5 mi. Turn Left on AGAWAM RD
Park at the entrance to the bog on the right taking care not to block the entrance. Approximate GPS address: 10 Agawam Road, Plymouth, MA

Features
Fawn Pond, Agawam River, Agawam Road, A. D. Makepeace bogs and reservoir; herring ladder in river; pines, bogs and ponds.
Fawn Pond[4] is a 33-acre (130,000 m^2) pond located south of Halfway Pond, northwest of Deer Pond, north of White Island Pond, northeast of Five Mile Pond, and east of Fearing Pond and Abner Pond, outside of the eastern boundary of Myles Standish State Forest. The outflow is a stream that flows into the Agawam River. Agawam River[4] is a stream (10+ miles long) is part of the Wareham River estuary. It was also formerly the name of the lower section of the Westfield River in western Massachusetts.

The river originates at Halfway Pond east of the Myles Standish State Forest and flows southwest through Glen Charlie Pond and East Wareham, and drains into the Wareham River near the center of Wareham. As the estuary's major contributor of nutrients and fresh water, the Agawam was one of the most important herring rivers in Massachusetts. Its herring runs have been operated by European settlers since 1632 and were officially established as a managed run in 1832.
Even today, it remains one of the few managed herring runs in Massachusetts, although few fish reach the river's spawning and nursery habitat. It includes 570 acres (2.3 km^2) of water bodies that could serve as habitat to alewife, blueback herring, and American shad. Approximately 36% of this habitat is in Halfway Pond. Fishway retrofit projects aim to restore river herring population to historic levels, perhaps as many as 100,000+ fish annually.
The Agawam River receives discharges from the Wareham Sewage Treatment plant, which discharges 0.76 million gallons per day of nitrogen-rich sewage effluent.
A.D. Makepeace see: http://www.admakepeace.com/

Difficulty
3.6 miles; 1hr 30 min; mostly on narrow sandy roads. Best done in dry weather.

Hike
Walk south on Agawam Road. When it split into Fawn Pond and Agawam Roads stay right and on Agawam Road. Follow it for over a mile. The power lines you pass under are about half way to Fawn Pond. When you come to a very steep hill stay right and bypass the hill. You will see a small bog ahead on the right and the Fawn Pond pumping station, a small gray building with green trim. Fawn Pond is ahead. There are trails all the way around Fawn Pond, but they are marked "NO Trespassing". This is due to Camp Squanto along its shores. Turn around and shortly after you pass the steep hill on the right there is a trail to the west side of the Makepeace bogs. Follow along the bogs on the west side to the reservoir and then along the reservoir. Cross under the power lines and then stay left as you go around the small bog. After you go around the western tip of the bog there will be a dirt road going up a small hill. It will merge with Fawn Pond Road heading north. Follow it to Agawam Road and to the car.

Small Pond with water lilies

Fawn Pond Pump House

Fawn Pond

Bog in the winter

Agawam Road to Fawn Pond

11.   A. K. Makepeace Bogs

Directions
Off Rt. 3, take Exit 3 towards Long Pond Road. Turn left onto Long Pond Rd - go 1.6 mi. Turn Right on Halfway Pond Rd - go 1.6 mi. Continue on Wareham Rd - go 0.3 mi. Arrive at 65 Wareham Rd, on the right.

Approximate GPS address: 65 Wareham Road, Plymouth, MA

Features
A. D. Makepeace Cranberry Bogs, Agawam River, Future site of River Run by
www.admakepeace.com
The Agawam River[4] is a stream (10+ miles long) in southeastern Massachusetts, and
is part of the Wareham River estuary.
The river originates at Halfway Pond east of the Myles Standish State Forest, runs
southwest through Glen Charlie Pond and East Wareham, and drains into the
Wareham River near the center of Wareham. As the estuary's major contributor of
nutrients and fresh water, the Agawam was one of the most important herring rivers
in Massachusetts. Its herring runs have been operated by European settlers since
1632 and were officially established as a managed run in 1832.
Even today, it remains one of the few managed herring runs in Massachusetts,
although few fish reach the river's spawning and nursery habitat. It includes
570 acres (2.3 km^2) of water bodies that could serve as habitat to ale wife, blue-black
herring, and American shad. Approximately 36% of this habitat is in Halfway Pond.
Fishway retrofit projects aim to restore river herring population to historic levels,
perhaps as many as 100,000+ fish annually.
This hike is around the perimeter of A. D. Makepeace bogs. Parts of the bogs have
been donated to the State of Massachusetts Trustee of Reservations in an
arrangement with A. D. Makepeace. Other portions will be developed by A. D.
Makepeace. What you will find after 2010 will be up to you to explore.

Difficulty
4.4 miles; 1:40 hrs.; very flat; easy walking.

Hike
After you turn into 65 Wareham Rd park on the right proceed on the grassy knoll
going south. Cross the bridge and then continue south along the west shore of the
reservoir. At the reservoir dam stay right and follow the large bog area around. You
will eventually come to a wodded peninsula that juts out into the bog. You will have
to go around it and then continue south on the right side of the bog. A little furthe
south the bogs narrow towards an abondened hous. Again stay right and continue
south to the very end of the bogs. Now return along the eastern edges of the bogs.
Initially follow on Wareham Road to the dirt road into the bog. Make a sharp right
and squezze around the gate. Follow the bogs til you get to the reservoir. Note
Agawam River on your left as you pass by.Cross over the dam. Note the fishladder
on the left after you cross. Now turn right and follow the road south-west back to the
bridge, cross and head south to your car.

Pond off bogs

Agawam River Reservoir

Agawam River Fish Ladder

A.D. Makepeace Bogs Trail

12.   White Island Bogs

Directions
Take exit 3 off Rt. 3 and head west towards Long Pond Road. Go left on LONG
POND RD - go 1.6 mi; turn Right on HALFWAY POND RD - go 1.6 mi; continue
on WAREHAM RD - go 0.71 mi. Arrive at 130 WAREHAM RD or by the power
lines
Approximate GPS directions: 130 Wareham Rd, Plymouth, MA

White Island Pond

Features
White Island Bogs, ponds colorful pump houses; Deer Pond; White Island Pond
Makepeace River Run. http://www.admakepeace.com/pages/real_estate/river_run-
plymouth.asp .
Most of the hike is on what will be Makepeace Rive Run Village property. To what
extend you will be able to hike in this area will depend on their progress and on No
Trespassing signage. There was none in May of 2010.
The White Island Pond can be found on the Sagamore USGS quad topo map. White
Island Pond is a reservoir at latitude and longitude coordinates of 41.8115, -70.6195,
and the altitude is 49 feet (15 meters).
Deer Pond is at coordinates of 41.8201, -70.6245, and the altitude is 56 feet (17
meters).

Difficulty
Easy hike; 3.4 miles; 1:25 hrs, flat

Pump Barker #12   **Pump Barker #10**

71

Hike

Park under the power lines, on either side of the road. Proceed east under the power lines for less than ¼ mile. Turn right onto a dirt trail heading south. It will come to a new road. Cross over it and continue south. When you reach the bogs stay to your left. At some point, you go around a small bay. Here take the trail up and through the woods till you reach White Island Pond. Turn right. At the pump station, turn right, and then left, when you can, along the south end of the bog. Pass a small bog on your left and then stay left till you reach Deer Pond. Turn around, head towards, and then pass the large sand area. Now stay left, follow the dirt road north. Cross the new road, and stay left again. This will bring you out at Wareham Rd. Turn right and the power lines and the car will be a few hundred feet on your right.

White Island Bog Trail

13.   Hedges Pond

Directions
From Rt. 3 take exit 3 to Long Pond Road. Go south on Long Pond Road. At one point Long Pond Road makes a right turn. If you go straight, you will be on Hedges Pond Road. Stay on Long Pond Road. It will turn into a dirt road. After about 1/2 mile, you will be at about 1001 Long Pond Road, where the town plans to build a parking lot. At the time of writing, there was no parking here. However, you can fit a car by one of the driveways. The trail starts about across from 1001 Long Pond Road.
Approximate GPS street address: 985 Long Pond Rd., Plymouth, MA

Hike Difficulty
About 2 miles, 45 minutes, flat around the pond.

Features
Hedges Pond; former Camp Dennen.[4]
Hedges Pond is a 26-acre pond located more than one mile north of Cedarville's business district past the Route 3 underpass, southeast of Black Jimmy Pond (Hyles Pond), and east of Little Herring Pond. Camp Dennen lies along the eastern shore of the pond. The 30-acre camp was formerly owned by The Episcopal Diocese of Massachusetts. The Town of Plymouth, along with a non-profit group called Friends

of Hedges Pond, has purchased the campsite as well 60 acres of land along the western shore of the pond to save the land from ever being developed.4
All the land around the pond is owned by the Town of Plymouth.

The Hike
The trail starts about across from 1001 Long Pond Road. Follow the trail straight east to the shore of the pond. As you come back up take a right to start your walk around the pond. Currently there are signs to the effect that the Camp Dennen facilities may not be used at this time. However, the trail will take you along the shore and through Camp Dennen. After Camp Dennen, the trail separates from the shoreline, but will bring you back to the starting point.

Sandy Beach   **Hedges Pond**

Toad on log   **Fall Colors**

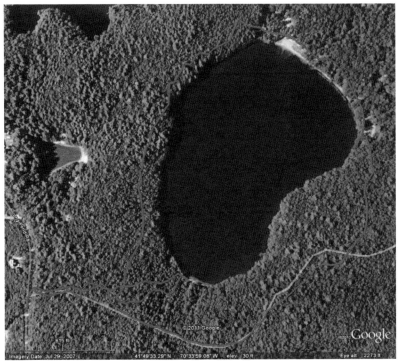

Hedges Pond Trail

14.   Pickerel Pond

Directions
Route 3 South to Exit 3-Clark Rd. Take a right at end of ramp onto Clark Rd. and
follow to stop sign. At stop sign take a left onto Long Pond Road and follow for 2.9
miles then take a right onto Lunn's Way. (Ponds of Plymouth) At 2nd stop sign turn
left onto Raymond Road (no street name sign here). Take your second left onto
Beatrice Ave. (follow blue sign to Pickerel Cove) Take first right onto Tadpole Lane
(again, sign to Pickerel Cove). Tadpole T's into Pioneer Trail. If you turn left and got
to the end of the cul-de-sac, you will see Wildlands Trust signs on trees to the right.
If you park there and make your way around the boulders and downed trees, you will
find yourself on a cart path leading down toward the pond.
Approximate GPS address: 195 Perseverance Path, Plymouth, MA

Features
Pickerel Pond, Triangle Pond, Little Herring Pond.
Pickerel Pond is located at latitude and longitude coordinates of 41.8209, -70.5825
and the altitude is 46 feet (14 meters).
Triangle Pond (Massachusetts) Coordinates 41°49'10"N 70°34'33"W.
Surface area   10 acres (4.0 ha); Settlements   Cedarville
Triangle Pond is a 10-acre pond in the Cedarville section located northwest of Great
Herring Pond, north of Island Pond, southwest of Little Herring Pond, and east of
Long Duck Pond.
All the land around the pond is owned by The Wildlands Trust. The bog area is
privately owned

Difficulty
2.6 miles, about 1 hr, 20 min., some bushwhacking, some hills.

| Pickerel in bloom | Pickerel Pond |

Hike
Start the hike by the rocks on the right of the cul-de-sac. Go around the rocks and
start to descent towards the pond. The trail narrows near the pond but continues
around the pond and reemerges near the parking area. You can now proceed about
2/3 around the cul-de-sac and bushwhack east till you reach Island Lake Road, about

600 feet. When you reach the road turn left, go to the next intersection and go right on Little Herring Pond Road. Triangle Pond will be on the right. Go about ¼ mile and turn left towards Little Herring Pond. When you reach the pond, look and then turn south and follow the trail. When you can turn left, follow the somewhat swampy trail till you overlook a cranberry bog area. This is a good place to turn around and make your way back to Little Herring Pond Road. Turn right/north on it and stay on it until Island Lake Road goes off to the left. Stay on it about 600 feet, until you can veer off to the right and reach a bog area. Follow the bog around on the right to were the dirt road veers to the left. Here turn right and head northwest until you reach the trail around the pond. You can get back to the parking area either by going right (shorter) or going left.

Triangle Pond   **Little Herring Pond**

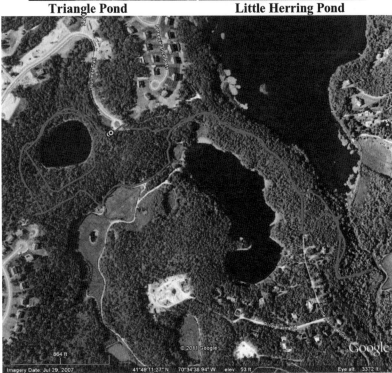

Pickerel Pond Hike

77

IV.   Myles Standish State Forest

The landscape of MSSF[4] is largely that of a pitch pine and scrub oak forest surrounding 16 lakes and ponds. Recreationally, Myles Standish State Forest is a Department of Conservation and Recreation state forest located in the towns of Plymouth and Carver in southeastern Massachusetts, approximately 45 miles (70 km) south of Boston. MSSF offers 26 sq. miles of camping, swimming, fishing, kayaking, canoeing and picnicking, fifteen miles (24 km) of paved bicycle trails, thirty-five miles (56 km) of horse trails and thirteen miles (21 km) of hiking trails. I advise getting a forest map at forest headquarters.

Hikes in Miles Standish State Forest:
1. Around College Pond
2. Charge Fearing Pond
3. Central MSSF and Fire Tower Hike
4. East Entrance Trail
5. Easthead Reservoir from Headquarters
6. Easthead Reservoir from P2
7. Federal and Rocky Pond
8. Lost Horse Bog
9. Three Cornered Pond

Distribution of hikes in Myles Standish State Forest

78

1.   Around College Pond
Directions and parking
From Rt. 3 Exit 5 go towards Long Pond Road. Go about two miles south on Long Pond Road to the entrance of Myles Standish State forest.
From Rt. 3, Exit 3 go about 3 miles north on Long Pond Road to the entrance of Myles Standish State forest.
Enter the park. Go about 1 ¾ miles to the first intersection. Turn left onto Upper College Pond Road. Go about 1 mile to the parking lot (P2 on park map) on the right by Three Cornered Pond Road.
Approximate GPS address Upper College Pond Rd., Plymouth, MA

Features
Small ponds, College Pond, tree lined dirt roads, wooded trails, and Myles Standish State Forest.
College Pond[4] is a 53-acre (210,000 m^2) natural kettlehole pond, located in the Myles Standish State Forest northeast of East Head Reservoir, Three Cornered Pond, New Long Pond and Barrett Pond, and north of Fearing Pond. There is a swimming beach and picnic area along the north shore of the pond.

Difficulty
5.1 miles; 2 hrs; no difficult terrain.

Hike
Start the hike in the northeast corner of the lot. Cross Three Cornered Pond Rd. TRhe trail starts a few feet west of Upper College Pond Road. Head northwest following the the blue markers. When you come to the open field stay right and then turn left near the end of the field. Again follow the blue markers. At the T s stay right. The trail will turn northwest again. After you turn right at the second intersection the trail will no longer be marked. At the next intersectioon make a sharp left and work your way around the small pond till you get to Lower College Pond Road. There is an opening to the right to go between two small ponds. The one on the left being Torrey Pond. At Lower College Pond Road make a right and follow the road a little less than ½ mile. Find the dirt road on the left, which eventually turns into Wayout Roasd.. Follow Wayout Road north to Howland Road. Follow Howland Road to Snake Hill Road. Turn right and stay right till you see Cranford Road on the left. There will be "cottages" visible along College Pond from this road. When Cranford Road turns west, stay left and come out onUpper College Pond Road. The parking lot is a few feet south.

Ponds along the trail

Howland Road   **Small Pond**

Trail around College Pond

80

Charge Pond

2. Charge and Fearing Pond

Directions and parking

From Rt. 3 Exit 5 go about two miles south on Long Pond Road to the entrance of Myles Standish State forest. From Rt. 3, Exit 3 go about three miles north on Long Pond Road to the entrance of Myles Standish State forest. Go about 1 ¾ miles to the first intersection. Turn left onto Upper College Pond Road. Go about 3 miles and turn left on Fearing Pond Road. Then turn left onto Charge Pond Road. There will be a parking area on the right about ½ mile west on Charge Pond Road
Approximate GPS address: 400 Charge Pond Rd., Plymouth, MA

Hike Difficulty

About 3.5 miles. 1:45 hours, not difficult. Some short hills around the ponds.

Features

Fearing Pond, Charge Pond, Grassy Pond, campgrounds, Old Stone fireplaces.
Charge Pond4 is a 23-acre warm water pond with an average depth of six feet and a maximum depth of 17 feet. It is located within a camping area in the southernmost section of Myles Standish State Forest, south of Fearing Pond, southwest of Abner Pond, and northwest of Little Long Pond. The pond is fed by groundwater and is the headwaters to Harlow Brook.
Fearing Pond4is a 24-acre (97,000 m^2) natural kettlehole pond with an average depth of ten feet and the maximum depth is 20 feet (6.1 m). It is located in the southern section of Myles Standish State Forest, north of Charge Pond, northwest of Abner Pond, west of Fawn Pond, south of College Pond, southeast of East Head Reservoir, and east of the forest headquarters. There is no direct access from the forest

81

headquarters as the bridge over the Wankinco River connecting Cranberry Road in Carver and Fearing Pond Road in Plymouth was washed out several years ago. The bridge has not been rebuilt. Camp Cachalot and Camp Squanto are nearby. The pond is fed by groundwater. A beach is located on the northern shore of the pond where boating access is as well. Summer cottages and campsites line the perimeter of the pond.

The Hike
From the parking lot, take the paved bicycle trail northwest. It will cross Southwest Line Rd and then Fearing Pond Road. Turn right, cross Circuit Road. After ~1/4 miles, you can leave the trail to the right and explore Fearing Pond. After you come back up to the road, turn right. Find the bike trail at the next street intersection (Doctors Pond Road) and follow it to the right. It will take you past Grassy Pond on the left. Continue to follow the bike trail south. It will pass a short cut to the parking lot. Continue till it ends in the campground off Charge Pond. Go down to Charge Pond. Now you can meander around Charge Pond, first along the shore, then along the road ending up on Charge Pond Road. You will find the parking lot ~ ¼ miles north up that road.

Old stone fire place

Fearing Pond

Grassy Pond

82

Charge and Fearing Ponds Walk

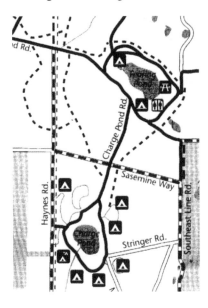

Pertinent Portion of Myles Standish State Forest Map

83

3.   Central MSSF and Fire Tower Hike

Directions
From Rt. 3, Exit go Right on CLARK RD. Turn Right on LONG POND RD - go 2.0 mi. Turn Left on ALDEN RD - go 1.4 mi. Continue on LOWER COLLEGE POND RD – about 4 miles, turn right onto Bare Hill Road, go about ½ mile, then turn left at the corner of Bare Hill and Three Cornered Pond Roads into the parking lot by the fire tower and park there.
GPS directions not available. Bare Hill Road, Plymouth, MA

Features
This is a quiet hike on dirt roads in the Forest. All woods, no bogs or ponds. Use a map obtainable at Forest Headquarters

Difficulty
4.2 miles; mostly flat; about 1:30 hours

Hike
From the parking lot, cross Bare Hill Road and turn left onto Kamesit Way. This is a straight dirt road heading north along a gas line easement. Go past Torrey Pond Rd, then Federal Pond Road, and turn right on Pokanoket Road. Go about ¾ mile east, then turn right onto Wayout Road. Follow it about ½ mile and then turn right on Federal Pond Road. After less than ½ mile turn left onto Sabbiatia Road. When it dead ends on Three Cornered Pond Road turn right and continue west to the fire tower and the parking lot.

Wintery Kamesit Way

Fire Tower

84

Fire Tower Trail

4. **East Entrance Trail**

Directions
From Rt. 3 Exit 5 go towards Long Pond Road. Go about two miles south on Long Pond Road to the entrance of Myles Standish State forest.
From Rt. 3, Exit 3 go about 3 miles north on Long Pond Road to the entrance of Myles Standish State forest.
Park in lot on right of entrance.
Approximate GPS address 391 Long Pond Road, Plymouth, MA

Features
Myles Standish State Forest; quiet wood trail and sandy road, no special features.
http://www.mass.gov/dcr/parks/southeast/mssf.htm

Difficulty
3.8 miles. 2:05 hrs, many short hills;

Hike
From Parking lot cross the street and start the hike on the bicycle path. Note the blue trail marker. After about a ½ mile look for the blue trail markers on the right and a trail on the left. Take the trail to the left or south. Follow the infrequent trail markers. The hiking trail marker is blue with an acorn or leaves. There is also a cross-country

ski marker. Follow both initially. After about another ½ mile the trail obviously splits. Take the trail to the left and follow it till you can see signs of civilization. After turning almost north the trail will turn south. Follow the trail markers to the right and then make a sharp right turn again away from the road. From here, the trail goes straight for over ½ mile. Just before you see the gate at Alden Road there will be blue markers on the left. Make a right onto the bicycle path at this point and follow it back to the parking lot.

Wintery Trails

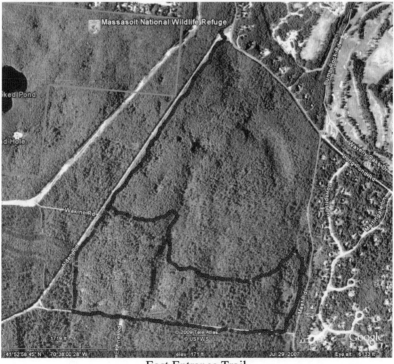

East Entrance Trail

5.   **East Head Reservoir from Forest Headquarters**

Directions and parking
From Rt.3 Exit 5 take Long Pond Road south to Myles Standish State Forest East Entrance. From exit 3 take Long Pond Road north. After entering Myles Standish State Forest, follow signs to Headquarters, ~five miles. Park in headquarters lower parking lot.
Approximate GPS address: Cranberry Rd & Lower College Pond Rd, S. Carver, Ma

Hike Difficulty
2.6 miles; 1:10 hours, flat, some short hills, marked trail

Features:
East Head Reservoir; beautiful pond, marked nature spots (brochure available at park headquarters).
East Head Reservoir4, also known as East Head Pond, is a 92-acre pond in Carver and Plymouth, within the Myles Standish State Forest, located northeast of the forest headquarters, east of Barrett Pond, southwest of New Long Pond and College Pond, and northwest of Fearing Pond. The reservoir is the headwaters to the Wankinco River.

The Hike
About the middle of the parking lot, there is a diagonal or northeast trail. Take it and follow it to a small peninsula. Then turn around and go to your right. The trail will follow the shore of the pond. Follow the blue triangle markers, which however go the other way. Near the northern end of the pond, the trail will emerge on College Pond Road only to go back after a few steps towards the pond on the right. In the western corner of the pond, the trail emerges on a power line trail. Follow the power lines to the right and after about 100 feet, there is a continuation of the trail to the right. Follow the trail mostly along the shoreline again to the southern point of the pond. Here the trail cuts over to the end of Fearing Pond Road. After crossing the reservoir dam, you will be back at the parking lot.

View of Pond

Outflow

87

Flow Control

East Head Reservoir Trail

6.   Easthead Reservoir from P2

Directions and parking
From Rt. 3 Exit 5 go towards Long Pond Road. Go about two miles south on Long Pond Road to the entrance of Myles Standish State forest.

From Rt. 3, Exit 3 go about 3 miles north on Long Pond Road to the entrance of Myles Standish State forest.
Enter the park. Go about 1 ¾ miles to the first intersection. Turn left onto Upper College Pond Road. Go about 1 mile to the parking lot (P2 on park map) on the right by Three Cornered Pond Road.
Approximate GPS address Upper College Pond Rd., Plymouth, MA

Features
Forest trail; Myles Standish State Forest; Easthead Reservoir; nature trail; Forest Headquarters
East Head Reservoir[4], also known as East Head Pond, is a 92-acre (370,000 m^2) pond in Carver and Plymouth, Massachusetts, within the Myles Standish State Forest, located northeast of the forest headquarters, east of Barrett Pond, southwest of New Long Pond and College Pond, and northwest of Fearing Pond. The reservoir is the headwaters to the Wankinco River.
The reservoir is a water supply for private bogs southwest of the headquarters.

Difficulty
5.2 miles; 2:15 hours; some moderately steep ups and downs from the parking lot to the reservoir; mostly flat around the reservoir.

Water Control

Overgrown area

Hike
Start the hike in the northwest corner of the parking lot, just to the left of the northern bulletin board. In general start out following the blue trail markers heading south west. Go right down the middle of the first meadow. Past the end make a slight left and turn south. After you cross Negas Road, dirt road, turn southwest again till you get to the next meadow. There take the trail to the right and into the woods. Follow it southwest till you get to the tip of a meadow and several intersecting trail. Continue straight to the dirt road and turn left. This will take you out to Halfway Pond Road. Cross and find a small trail to the left of the telephone pole. Follow it to the clearing for the electric lines. Turn right and search for a trail to the left towards the reservoir. If you get to the road you went too far. Follow the trail around the reservoir clockwise. Near the park headquarters the trail emerges on a road and you need to cross the outflow from the reservoir on the road. At this point you may visit the headquarters or continue following the trail clockwise around the reservoir again.

At some point the trail emerges on the road again, but shortly continues on around the reservoir on a nice trail. This portion has several boardwalk sections. When you get to the electric line clearings turn right and look for the small trail on the left that will take you back to Halfway Pond Road. You can also turn left and then right on Halfway Pond Road. At the telephone pole with the trail cross and retrace your steps back to the car.

Parking Lot #2 to Easthead Reservoir and back

7.   Federal and Rocky Ponds

Directions
From Rt. 3 Exit 3gto west on Clark Road to Long Pond Road. Turn right and go about 2 miles to Myles Standish State Forest Entrance. This is Alden Road.
It turns into Lower College Pond Road. After about 4 miles from the entrance, make a right onto Bare Hill Road. After about 1 ½ miles you come to Federal Pond Road. Just beyond Federal Pond Road on the left, there is an area suitable for parking.

Features
Federal Cranberry Bogs, Federal and Rocky ponds, pines,
Federal Pond is a 129-acre (0.52 km^2) pond in Carver and Plymouth, Massachusetts. A small portion of the northeastern shore of the pond is in the Myles Standish State Forest. The pond is located southwest of Rocky and Curlew Ponds, and northeast of Dunham Pond. Two unnamed islands lie in the middle of the pond. The water quality is impaired due to non-native aquatic plants and non-native fish species.
The only road leading to the pond, Old Federal Road in Carver, is a private road. As such, the pond is officially off limits to the public, although a high-tension line right of way crosses the northern tip of the pond and is frequented by sport fishermen.

90

Rocky Pond is an 18-acre (73,000 m^2) pond in the Myles Standish State Forest. The pond is located south of Curlew Pond.

Difficulty
5.2 miles; 2 hrs, some short hills.

Hike
From the parking area, walk back to Federal Pond Road, and turn right/west. Follow the sandy road till you get to another dirt road, West Line Rd. Here turn left and shortly again right. Walk down and take in the view of the large bog area, Federal Bogs, and the farmhouse across the bogs. Beyond here, everything is private. So, turn around go back to West Line Road and turn left. Follow West Line Road for a little over a mile. Then take a smaller trail to the left. It will take you to the power lines and the northeast tip of Federal Pond. A few feet east along the power lines, a trail goes off to the left. Follow it in the woods in the direction of the power lines. After a little more than ¼ mile take a trail going northwest away from the power lines. It will bump into Rocky Pond Rd. Turn right and follow Rocky Pond Rd till you get to a bog area on the right. Follow the road to the end of the bog than turn right and follow the edge of the bog. Make a sharp right and continue to follow the bog till you see Rocky Pond on the left and another bog area on the right. Follow the edge of the bog to its south corner and then take a path up to and across the power lines, up to Bare Hill Rd. Go south on Bare Hill Rd. Look for the bicycle trail on the left. Cross over to it when you can and follow it to Federal Pond Rd, turn right, go to Bare Hill Rd and make another right and the car will be just on the left.

| House on Bog | Federal Pond |

| Pump House | Rocky Pond |

Federal & Rocky Ponds Trail

8.   Lost Horse Bog

Directions and parking
From Rt. 3 Exit 5 go towards Long Pond Road. Go about two miles south on Long Pond Road to the entrance of Myles Standish State forest.
From Rt. 3, Exit 3 go about 3 miles north on Long Pond Road to the entrance of Myles Standish State forest.
Enter the park. Go about 1 ¾ miles to the first intersection. Continue straight on Lower College Pond Road. Go almost 3 miles then make a right onto Halfway Pond Road. There is a sign pointing to the equestrian parking lot (P3 on the Forest map). Follow the signs to Equestrian Parking Lot (P3) at Jessup Rd and Halfway Pond Rd.

Features
Quiet dirt roads through the woods leading to a quiet isolated bog. Lost Horse Bog. Myles Standish State Forest.
http://www.wickedlocal.com/plymouth/news/x1985977218/Little-known-area-of-Myles-Standish-State-Forest-catches-attention-of-the-state

Difficulty
5.2 miles on flat dirt roads, some gradual uphill and downhill; narrow trail around the bog. About 2 hrs.

Hike
From the parking lot go back out to HALFWAY Pond Road and turn left/west. Continue due west. Cross Dunham, Road, and then West Line Road. Continue to Shaw Road. (All about ½ mile apart, all are marked with red forest signs.) Make a right onto Shaw Road, then turn left onto Ryan Road. Near the end of Ryan Road, before you get to the houses, make a left onto a smaller road going southeast, which leads to the bog. You may hike around the bog and retrace your steps back to the car. Or, from the east corner of the bog bushwhack east out to Shaw Road. Turn right and make your way back to Halfway Pond Road. Turn left and make your way back to the car.

Lost Horse Bog

Water Supply

Bog and Water Supply

Haircap moss (Polytrichum)

Lost Horse Bog from Equestrian parking Lot, P3

9.   Three Cornered Pond

Directions and parking
From Rt. 3 Exit 5 go towards Long Pond Road. Go about two miles south on Long
Pond Road to the entrance of Myles Standish State forest.
From Rt. 3, Exit 3 go about 3 miles north on Long Pond Road to the entrance of
Myles Standish State forest.
Enter the park. Go about 1 ¾ miles to the first intersection. Turn left onto Upper
College Pond Road. Go about 1 mile to the parking lot (P2 on park map) on the right.
Approximate GPS address: Upper College Pond Rd., Plymouth, MA

Hike Difficulty
4.1 miles, 1:40 hrs, some hills.
Features
New Long Pond, Three Cornered Pond, Round Pond, ponds, and pines.
New Long Pond[4] is a 23-acre pond in the Myles Standish State Forest located
northeast of East Head Reservoir and southwest of College Pond and Three-
Cornered Pond. The water quality is impaired due to non-native aquatic plants.
Three Cornered Pond[4] is a 14-acre pond in the Myles Standish State Forest located
northeast of New Long Pond and southwest of College Pond. The water quality is
also impaired due to non-native aquatic plants.

The Hike

Secure a park map at headquarters. The trail starts in the southwest corner of the parking lot and goes south from there parallel to the road. When you get to Halfway Pond Road, make a right. Follow the road for about ¼ mile and look for the trail on the right. Follow the trail to a dirt road, Negus Rd, turn right. Go about ¼ miles. Look for the trail markers on the left. Take the trail across Three Cornered Pond Road to a corner of Three-Cornered Pond. Bear right, go past Round Pond. After the pond, about ¼ mile, make a sharp right; then a sharp left following the trail markers. At the open field stay to your left and make a left down the hill again following the trail markers. Past the bottom of the hill the trail make a sharp right. Going straight would take you to College Pond. Follow the trail to the open field entering on the north corner. Follow the field around on the left and then find the trail at the south corner of the field. The trail will take you back to the parking lot.

New Long Pond

Three Cornered Pond

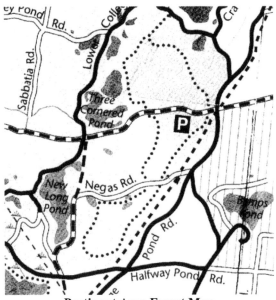

Pertinent Area Forest Map

95

Frank Werny

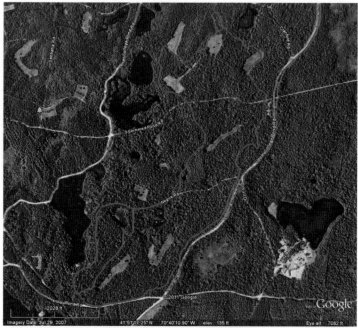

Three Cornered Pond Hike

V.   **Off Hwy 3 A**

Location of Hikes

1.   **Center Hill Conservation Area**
2.   **Ellisville**
3.   **Wynn Reservation**
4.   **Sagamore Hill/Scusset Beach**

1. Center Hill Conservation Area
Former Joslin Diabetic Foundation Camp, now the town's newly dedicated Center Hill Conservation Area.

Directions
From Hwy 3 Exit 2, go east. Turn left onto 3A, go about 2miles, past Ellisville State Park, and turn left into the southern entry to Center Hill Road. There will be two town parking lots with split rail fencing. The first one on the right and another on the left. The one on the right gives easy access to the beach. The one on the left gives access to the western portion of the conservation area.
Approximate GPS address 175 Center Hill Rd, Plymouth, MA

Hike difficulty
2.6 miles; about 1.5 hrs, mostly flat, some sandy walking on the beach.

Features
Sandy Beach; Center Hill Pond; bog; Cape Cod Bay, bay views; beach walk, walk in the pines.

The Hike
Western Hike
From the west parking lot make your way to the dirt road to the west of the parking lot and turn left. Follow this road until it comes to a bog area. Follow around the bog with the bog to your right. In the north corner, take the trail going north. Keep going north till the trail makes a sharp left and then tow rights. It will now continue south till it comes out on the dirt road you started on. Turn left and it will take you back to near the parking lot.

Beach Hike
From the beach parking lot walk north on the road. At the first driveway turn right and walk up the hill to the house. Pass the house on the right, and just before you are past the house, there is a trail to the right, that will take to a beach overlook. At the beach overlook take a trail to the left and after a while turn right and go back to the house, or you can go directly back to the house from the overlook. About 100 feet southwest of the house there is a trail to the left. It will take you to the beach. After about 400 feet of open area and low growth, just before the pond, there is a trail to the right, which leads back to the parking lot. However, you can continue south for another ¼ mile on the beach. Before you get to the end of the public beach there is a trail to the southern tip of Center Hill Pond and a nice view of the pond.

Southern End of Beach   Northern End of Beach

Southern End of Center Hill Pond

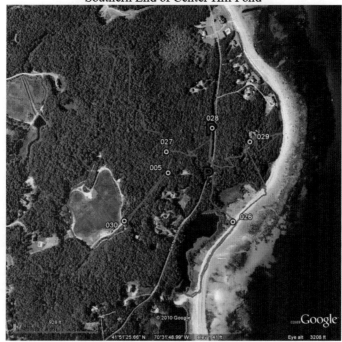

Center Hill Area Trails

Frank Werny

2.   Ellisville State Park and Beach
Ellisville Harbor State Park
Rte 3A, Plymouth
508 866-2580

Directions and parking
Take Rt. 3 to Exit 2 and turn east to Hwy 3A. Turn north or left onto Hwy 3A. Go about 2 miles. Pass Old Sandwich Rd on left and Ellisville Harbor State Park will be on the right. Proceed to parking lot.
Approximate GPS address 1890 State Rd, Plymouth, MA

Hike Difficulty
Easy hike; about 2.4 miles, 1:05 hr., depending on the seasonal beach contour; one set of stairs.

Features:
Wooded trail; rocky beach; sandy beach, tidal marshes, tidal run-off, salt pond, views of Ellisville Harbor.
Ellisville Harbor[4] is a unique coastal property, including an 18th century farmstead, beachfront, salt marsh, rolling meadows, and red pine forest. It is also one of the most scenic spots on the South Shore coastline, where you can see small fishing boats, a barrier beach, and sphagnum bog, forested upland and open meadows. Recreation activities include walking, bird watching, beach combing, and sightseeing. In fall and winter, harbor seals can often be seen just offshore. Between 2,500 and 5,000 years ago, prehistoric Native Americans hunted, fished, harvested shellfish, and made tools here. The park was once part of the Harlow family farmstead.

99

Ellisville[4] is a village located on Cape Cod Bay, and is situated south of Vallerville and north of Cedarville. The neighborhoods within Ellisville include Harlow's Landing and Eastland Heights. Ellisville Harbor, in the northern part of the village, boasts a natural harbor and beach.

Ellisville Harbor

Walk by an abandoned Christmas tree farm on your way to the rocky coastline. Ellisville Harbor State Park is one of the lesser-known parks in Massachusetts, but if you love beachcombing and watching seals, it will soon become one of your favorites. Located at the southern end of the town of Plymouth, the park spans 101 acres of meadow, woodlands, salt marsh, and shore. (by www.Trails.com)

The Hike

Follow the trail from the north end of the parking lot. It parallels Davis Road or Grace's Lane. It will cross a road by the small ranger station and then head towards the bay. Go down the steps and turn south or right. Follow the beach as far south as you can, about a mile. The southern tip of the peninsula is forever shifting and may not look like it did on the attached map. As you can see, the trail on the map did not follow the outlines on the Google map. Now turn right and follow the tidal water run-off north. As the run-off turns west, you can take a trail on the west side of the overgrown sand dune. At one point the trail runs out and you can take one of the small trails back to the beach and head back to the steps and follow the trail to the parking area.

Tidal Flats

Mind the Birds

Ellisville Harbor Trail

3. Richard F. Wynn Memorial Reservation

Directions
Rt. 3 to Exit 2 to 3A north. Go about 2 miles north.
Turn left into Indian Head Trailer Park Resort. Park near entrance to resort.
Start the hike on Bay Hill Road.
Approximate GPS address: 30 Bog Hill Rd, Ellisville, MA

Hike Difficulty
2.8 miles, 1:10 hours, some short steep hills on the Wildlands Trust portion.

Features
Working bog, Savery Pond; R. F. Wynn Memorial Reservation; quiet pine forest;
some Rt. 3 noise.

Hike
Bay Hill Road is marked private but may be used as access to the Richard F. Wynn
Memorial Reservation. Start on that road just short of the resort entrance. Walk by a
working bog and then by Savery Pond on your right. At the dirt road junction make a
sharp left and go southwest. Look for and pass a stone marker on your right, R. F.

Wynn Memorial Reservation, marked oo4 on map. Just when you can see a paved road up ahead (Quail Run) the trail into the Wildlands Trust area starts on your right. Follow it a while to the first clear trail junction (marker 006 on map) and stay to your right there. The trail will make a circle and emerge on the original trail (marker 007 on map). Turn left and follow the trail back to the dirt road. Turn left on the dirt road and it will take you back to your car parked near the resort entrance.

Wynn Reservation Marker

Harvesting Cranberries

Savory Pond

Green Cranberries

Richard F. Wynn Memorial Reservation Hike

4.   **Sagamore Hill, Scusset Beach**

Directions and parking
Take Rt. 3 south to Exit 1 and exit to Scusset Beach Road. Follow the road east to
State Park Entrance. Park in the next parking lot to the right after the office parking
lot.
Approximate GPS street address: 250 Scusset Beach Rd., Sagamore, MA

Hike Difficulty
2.2 or 5 miles. Some minor hills. 1:55 hrs,

Features
Sagamore Hill; Tuppers Creek Marsh; Scusset Beach; Cape Cod Bay; Sagamore Hill
Military Reservation; Cape Cod Canal. The first 2.2 miles are through the woods and
then it is down to the beach and along Cape Cod Canal.
Sagamore Hill Military Reservation[4]
Sandwich is the site of the Cape Cod Bay entrance to the Cape Cod Canal. The
northern point of Sandwich, where Sagamore Hill and the Scusset Beach State
Reservation lie, is divided from the rest of the town by the canal.
Camp Candoit Sagamore, Massachusetts
Type: Coastal Defense
Coordinates: W 41.7773, -70.5031944
Built by United States Army1940s. In use 1941-1945

103

Current owner: Massachusetts, Controlled by United States Army Garrison,
Occupants: 241st Coast Artillery, Battery C
Sagamore Hill Military Reservation was a coastal defense site located in Sagamore.
Built on state land its mission was to protect the Cape Cod Canal from possible air
and naval attack. It never did have to fire its guns though but it did play an important
part in the defense of the canal. The Panama mounts (1942) and battery commander's
station of a two-gun 155mm battery still remain here, as well as several magazine
igloos.

The Hike
2.2 or 5 miles all about Sagamore Hill, Scusset Beach and along the Cape Cod
Canal. From the parking lot, use the crosswalk to cross over to the gated beginning
of the trail. Take the left branch and stay on it, staying to the left till you get to the
covered igloo entrances and the gun emplacement. The top of the hill is just ahead
and does offer a view of the bay. Turn around and follow the trail back, but stay left.
Turn left at the first and second trail junctions. Follow the trail to the end where it
narrows considerably before it gets to Tuppers Creek Marsh. At the T, you can turn
right and follow the narrow trail between the woods and the marsh. At some point,
you have to turn around and follow the trail back. On your way back, stay left again,
all the way back to the gate. To here, it is approximately 2.2 miles. You can now
continue and do another 2.5 mile circle. Turn left and walk down the road till you get
to the beach parking lot (~1 mile), and cross over the dune between the two beach
pavilions. On the beach turn right and walk to the canal jetty. Here turn right again,
make your way up to the canal road and follow it till you are at the fishing pier and
your car will be on the right.

View from Sagamore Hill

Tuppers Creek Marsh

Empty Scusset Beach

North End of Cape Cod Canal

104

5-mile hike

VI.   Plymouth Parks Area
The area is bordered by Wareham in the west, by Bourne Road in the east, by
Ezekiels Pond in the north, and by Rt. 25 in the south. A small portion extends
beyond Rt. 25 to the Barnstable County border. The Plymouth 1000Acre area at one
time consisted of 5 'Parks'. They were New England Park, Woodmere Park,
Smithsonian Park, Bournehurst Park, and Sandy Lake Park. In the early 1900 these
were privately owned by several owners and 7000 small lots were being sold by
these owners mainly for camping. In the 1930s the town started acquiring the large
and small parcels. Some of the titles are still in dispute. All trace of these parks have
disappeared if they ever existed beyond the maps. White Island Pond Road, a dirt
trail at this time, cuts through the area.
The green area on the map was designated as 'Sandy Lake Park', the pink area east
of White Island Pond Road was Bournehurst Park, the yellow area on the eastern
border was New England Park, and the blue and orange areas between were
Smithsonian Park and Woodmere Park. Three of the larger owners were Colonial
Land Co of Lynn, MA (Bournehurst Park), F. I. Haswell of Danvers, MA
(Woodmere Park), and F. I. Haswell and G. A. De Land (Sandy Lake Park)

105

The five "parks" of the 1,000 acres property are New England Park, Woodmere Park, Smithsonian Park, Bournehurst Park and Sandy Lake Park.

Distribution of Hikes

Frank Werny

The hikes:
1. Century Bogs
2. Horse Pond
3. Red Brook
4. Weeks Pond

1. Century Bogs

Directions
From Exit 3 Rt. 3 go west on Clark Rd
Turn LEFT on LONG POND RD go 1.63 mi
Turn RIGHT on HALFWAY POND RD go 1.62 mi
Continue on WAREHAM RD go about 9 miles
Turn left on Access Rd
Turn LEFT on BARKER RD; go a little less than a mile
Arrive at 263 BARKER RD, WAREHAM, Park in open area on right.
Approximate GPS address: 263 Barker Rd, Wareham, MA

Features
Bogs; ponds; Century Bogs; Bartlett Pond
http://www.wickedlocal.com/plymouth/news/enviroment/x562895137/Makepeace-aids-conservation
Commonly known as the Century Bog, the property consists of 176 acres in Wareham and 69 acres in Plymouth, beginning at the southern end of White Island Pond and linking to MassWildlife's 673-acre Red Brook Wildlife Management Area. Red Brook is a small, spring-fed, cold-water coastal stream that flows roughly 4.5 miles from its headwaters in Plymouth through several former cranberry bogs to the ocean. The Red Brook Wildlife Management Area is adjacent to the Trustees of Reservations' 210-acre Lyman Reserve.
With the Century Bog acquisition complete, 883 acres of contiguous land are permanently protected. The acquired property also includes several run-of-river cranberry bogs, wooded pitch pine and scrub oak upland and the 11-acre Bartlett Pond.

Water Flow Control

Pickerels in the bog

107

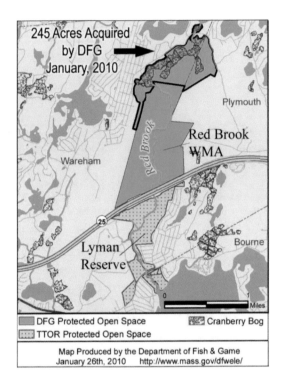

Difficulty
3.7 miles. 1 hr 45 mi. Flat hike around the bogs;

Hike
From the open area where you parked, turn right and continue along the perimeter of the bogs. After about ¾ of a mile you will reach Bartlett Pond. Turn left and then stay right going along the south shore of Bartlett Pond. Almost at the northern tip you will have to turn around, and come back to the bog area. Once you emerge from the trees stay right. After about 500 feet you will come to the spot where Red Brook flows out of the bogs to the southeast. Here you can take a trail to the northwest through the woods or continue around the perimeter of the bogs, keeping them to your left. Continue for almost a mile till the dirt road turns right towards a small dead end bog. Here you may choose to include that small bog, or cut it off by heading across the opening and again following the bog till you reach a road, Barker/White Island Pond Road. Turn left. Follow the road a few steps and turn left again along the bog. Again follow the bog till you are heading southwest and can no longer pursue a trail. Turn right and head out to Barker Road Turn left. On your right across some conservation land you can view White Island Pond. After a few steps south on Barker Road you can again go off road towards the bog and follow the trail to the right back to the parking area.

Century Bogs Trail

Water Flow form White Island Pond to the bogs   Bartlett Pond

109

Pump Station

Other options:
See following map.
You can start at the end of Dana Lane, Wareham, MA. Turn east into the forest and then turn north or left, and follow the trail to Bartlett Pond and then follow the previous hike instructions. About 4.3 miles.
Driving instructions: From Exit 3 Route 3 turn west then turn Left on LONG POND RD - go 1.6 mi. Turn Right on HALFWAY POND RD. Go 1.6 miles. Turn left on Wareham Rd. Go about 9 miles. Turn Right on DOUGLAS LN Turn Left on DANA LN - go 0.2 mi
Arrive at 98 DANA LN, EAST WAREHAM,

Or, you can start just to the right or east of 236 Bournehurst Drive, on the long abandoned White Island Pond Road. It is now a dirt road and will take you all the way to Barker Road (about 1 ¼ miles), where you can join the initial hike route. About 6.5 miles.
Or you can turn sharp left after about 0.75 miles on White Island Pond Road and follow a trail west towards the bogs. About 6.1 miles.
Directions to 236 Bournehurst Drive:
 From Exit 3 Route 3 turn west then turn Left on LONG POND RD - go 1.6 mi. Turn Right on HALFWAY POND RD - go 0.7 mi. Turn Left on BOURNE RD - go 4.9 mi. Turn Right on WHITE ISLAND POND RD - go 0.2 mi. Continue on BOURNEHURST DR - go 0.2 mi. Turn Right on CABOT CIR - go 0.1 mi
Turn Left on BOURNEHURST DR - go 0.3 mi. Arrive at 236 BOURNEHURST DR, PLYMOUTH, on the Right.

2.   Horse Pond

Directions and parking
From Rt.3 Exit 3 take Long Pond Road south to Half Way Pond Road. Turn right and follow to Bourne Road on left. Go about 5 miles on Bourne Road till you get to get to the power lines just before the Hwy 25 overpass. Park along the road near the power lines.
Approximate GPS street address 970 Bourne Rd, Plymouth, MA

Hike Difficulty
2 miles, 1 hour15 min., flat

Features
No special features except Horse Pond. Quiet walk in the woods.

The Hike
Start the hike by going east along the power lines for about ½ miles. After the power lines make a slight southeasterly turn there will be a trail to the left. You will pass Horse Pond to your right. Just follow the trail. It will bring you out on Bourne Road. Your car will be a little over ¼-mile to the left or south.

Boulder in the pines

Horse Pond

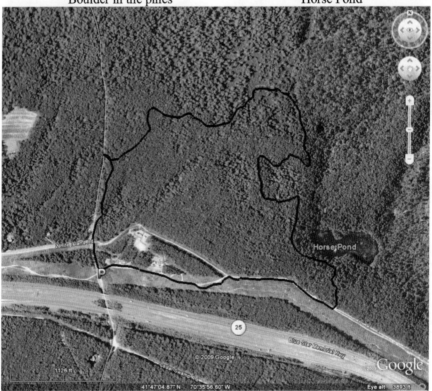
Horse Pond Trail

112

3.   Red Brook Creek

Directions
From Rt.3 Exit 3 take Long Pond Road south to Half Way Pond Road. Turn right and follow to Bourne Road on left. Go about 5 miles on Bourne Road till you get to get to the power lines just before the Hwy 25 overpass. Park along the road near the power lines just before the underpass for Rt.25.
Approximate GPS street address 970 Bourne Rd, Plymouth, MA

Features
A portion of the hike is along Red Brook Creek; Garland Cranberry Bog; forest. Former Sandy Lake Park area.

Difficulty
3.8 miles; 1:30 hrs; mostly flat

Hike
Start the hike by following the poer lines west. At the junction of the power and gas lines and the road take the dirt road to the very left and continue to follow it past the bog. It turns into a forest trail and then makes a right turn away from the hwy and into the woods. After a short distance you can see Red Brook on the left. Continue the meandering trail keeping to the left. Once you can see the power lines and Red Brook again, cross the power line clearing and follow the trail north. It is following Red Brook. When you reach the bridge you have also reached a gas line clearing. Crossing the bridge and following the power lines would get you Standish Avenue in Wareham. Crossing the bridge and following the trail on the right would lead to Bartlett's Pond on the south end of Century Bogs.
From the bridge turn back and follow the gas lines to the road. Cross the road and continue to follow the gasline clearing till you get to what appears to be an electric fence. Turn right and make your way out to the road. Follow it to the poerlines and then follow the power lines back to the car.

Water Supply

Garland Bog

113

Red Brook   Bridge across Red Brook

4.   Weeks Pond

Directions

From Exit 3 Rt. 3 turn west. Turn Left on LONG POND RD - go 1.6 mi
Turn Right on HALFWAY POND RD - go 0.7 mi. Turn Left on BOURNE RD - go
5.1 mi. Arrive at 1010 BOURNE RD, PLYMOUTH, a gas line access on the left
Park on the gas line right of way without blocking their access.
Approximate GPS address 1010 Bourne Lane, Plymouth, MA 02360

Features
Weeks Pond, Nye Reservoir, GARLAND NYE REALTY TRUST, 620 HEAD OF THE BAY RD, BUZZARDS BAY, MA 02532; New England Park, bogs, ponds, pines

Difficulty
Flat 3.2 miles, 1:15 hrs. Trail crosses Nye Bogs, which may be posted No Trespassing. (Most cranberry companies allow walkers when there is no commercial activity in the bog, such as in winter.).

Hike
From the parking spot cross the street and proceed west around the gate and follow the gas line right of way through part of New England Park, till you get to the highway rest stop area. Follow the perimeter on the left till you reach the guard rail on the left. Turn into the woods just before the rail and head to the gate in the fence. Go thru and turn left or south. Follow that trail for over a mile. Pass Weeks Pond and then the Nye Reservoir and reach the Nye bogs owned by GARLAND NYE REALTY TRUST. Stay to your right, unless you want to add some distance, in which case you could go left and walk around the whole bog. When you can, turn right again along the edge of the woods, and emerge by a small bog. Continue to the larger bog area and then stay left. When you can turn west and make your way up to Morning Mist Lane, also known as Old Man's Path. Turn right and continue on Morning Mist Lane to the circle. Pass the house and enter the bog straight ahead. Make a right about 100 feet into the bog on the dirt road. Follow that path to the fence along the highway. At the fence follow it sharp right till it ends and you can go sharp left to the highway and then follow the shoulder for a few yards to the rest stop. Continue east in the rest stop till the exit ramp separates and to the right of the exit you get to a slight slope on the east side, which is the gas line and where you came from. Follow the path back to the car.

Weeks Pond

115

Nye Reservoir

Trail Map

VII.   Plymouth

Plymouth[4] (historically also known as Plimouth and Plimoth) is a town in Plymouth County, Massachusetts, United States and is the largest municipality in Massachusetts by area. The population was 51,701 at the 2000 census, with an estimated 2008 population of 58,379. Plymouth is one of two county seats of Plymouth County, the other being Brockton. It is named after Plymouth, Devon, England, which is, in turn, named after its location at mouth of the River Plym. Plymouth is best known for being the landing site of the *Mayflower* and the Pilgrims. Founded in 1620, Plymouth is the oldest municipality in New England and one of the oldest in the United States. It also is the oldest continually inhabited English settlement in the modern United States. The town has served as the location of several prominent events, the most notable being the First Thanksgiving feast.

Plymouth served as the capital of Plymouth Colony from its founding in 1620 until the colony's dissolution in 1691.
Plymouth is located approximately 40 miles (63.4 kilometers) south of Boston in a region of Massachusetts known as the South Shore. Throughout the 19th century, the town thrived as a center of rope making, fishing, and shipping, and once held the world's largest rope making company, the Plymouth Cordage Company. While it continues to be an active port, today the major industry of Plymouth is tourism. Plymouth is served by Plymouth Municipal Airport, and contains Pilgrim Hall Museum, the oldest continually operating museum in the United States.
As one of the country's first settlements, Plymouth is well known in the United States for its historical value. The events surrounding the history of Plymouth have become part of the mythology of the United States, particularly those relating to Plymouth Rock, the Pilgrims, and the First Thanksgiving.

The Hikes (north to south):
1. **Russell/Sawmill pond**
2. **Plymouth Rock to Cordage**
3. **Morton Park Ponds**
4. **Plymouth Rock to Billington Sea (Pilgrim Trail)**
5. **Crawley Woods**
6. **Plymouth Long Beach**
7. **Town Forest**
8. **South Triangle Pond**

Distribution of the Hikes near town

117

1.   Sawmill and Russell's Pond

Directions
Take Rt. 3 Exit #6 towards Plymouth Ctr./Samoset St go 0.6 mi
Turn Left on Standish Ave. - go 1.5 mi
Turn Left on Bourne St. Go to end of Bourne St where road splits.
Approximate GPS directions: 57 Bourne Street, Plymouth, Ma

Features
Short hike in North Plymouth; Mill Pond; Russell's Pond Russell – Sawmill Ponds
Conservation Area
This area is the largest tract of Town owned land in North Plymouth. The Town
purchased the majority of the 64-acre parcel in 1969. Mature trees, a perennial
stream, ponds, and trails through the valleys and hills make for interesting hiking,
picnicking and fishing. .

Difficulty
Almost two miles (1.8); 45 minutes; some short hills

Hike
Park on the left just before the road splits. Turn right and go past the east end of
Sawmill Pond. Follow the dirt path between the ponds and then staying left to the
end of the path. You can cross the barrier at the end of the path, but at the next
barrier turn around and retrace your steps along the path. After the open area the path
will make a sharp right. Take the first obvious trail to the left heading west into the
forest. Follow it till you can make another left into a depressed trail. Follow it out to
Rt. 3. Make a right into the open area and follow the electric lines to the point where
they split and one branch goes right. Look for a trail to the left. Follow it almost back
to the trail you went out on, but turn left just before and head up the hill. This will
take you along the top of a small ridge where you can get nice views of the west end
of Russell's Pond before you join the dirt path and turn left to get back to the car.

Depressed Trail

Sawmill Pond

Russell Sawmill Ponds Trail

2.   Plymouth Rock to Cordage Center

Directions and parking
From Rt. 3 take Exit 6 towards Plymouth. Stay on Samoset Street, Cross Rt. 3A and
continue to the rotary near the waterfront. Go right and park near Plymouth Rock.
Approximate GPS street address: 45 Water St., Plymouth, MA

Hike Difficulty
3.8 miles, 1.5 hours, very flat

Features
Plymouth Rock, Plymouth waterfront, Plymouth Coastline, Mayflower, Nelson Park,
Cordage site.

Mayflower[4]
The *Mayflower* was the famous ship that transported the English Separatists, better
known as the Pilgrims, from Southampton, England, to Plymouth, Massachusetts
(which would become the capital of Plymouth Colony), in 1620.[1]
The vessel left England on September 6 (Old Style)/September 16 (New Style),[2]
and after a grueling 66-day journey marked by disease, which claimed two lives, the
ship dropped anchor inside the hook tip of Cape Cod (Provincetown Harbor) on
November 11/November 21.[1] The *Mayflower* originally was destined for the mouth

Mayflower in Plymouth Harbor by **William Halsall (1882)**

of the Hudson River, near present-day New York City, at the northern edge of England's Virginia colony, which itself was established with the 1607 Jamestown Settlement.[3] However, the *Mayflower* went off course as the winter approached, and remained in Cape Cod Bay. On March 21/28, 1621, all surviving passengers, who had inhabited the ship during the winter, moved ashore at Plymouth, and on April 5/15, the *Mayflower,* a privately commissioned vessel, returned to England.[1] In 1623, a year after the death of Captain Christopher Jones, the *Mayflower* was most likely dismantled for scrap lumber in Rotherhithe, London.[4]

The *Mayflower* has a famous place in American history as a symbol of early European colonization of the future US. With their religion oppressed by the English Church and government, the small party of religious separatists who comprised about half of the passengers on the ship desired a
life where they could practice their religion freely. This symbol of religious freedom resonates in US society and the story of the Mayflower is a staple of any American history textbook. Americans whose roots are traceable back to New England often believe themselves to be descended from *Mayflower* passengers.

The main record for the voyage of the Mayflower and the disposition of the Plymouth Colony comes from William Bradford who was a guiding force and later the governor of the colony.

Plymouth Cordage Company4 was a rope making company located in Plymouth, Massachusetts. The company, founded in 1824, had a large factory located on the Plymouth waterfront. By the late 19th century, the Plymouth Cordage Company had become the largest manufacturer of rope and twine in the world.[1] The company specialized in ship rigging, and was chosen among other competitors in the early 1900s to manufacture the rope used on the USS Constitution.

The Plymouth Cordage Company served as the largest employer in Plymouth for over 100 years. It went out of business in 1964 after over 140 years of continuous operation. By the early 1960s, the company could no longer withstand competition from more advanced synthetic-fiber ropes, and subsequently declared bankruptcy. It was bought out by the Columbian Rope Company in 1965.[2] Parts of the original machinery are now on display at Mystic Seaport in Mystic, Connecticut.

Cordage Commerce Center[4]

Wide view of the Cordage Factory, with the prominent smokestack to the left. In modern times, the 45-acre Cordage factory property in North Plymouth has been turned into a large retail and office center. The building, now known as *Cordage Commerce Center*, houses the Plymouth MBTA station, a terminus for the Old Colony Line. The factory also contains several restaurants, offices, and stores. University of Massachusetts Boston currently offers some classes in a wing of the building. The largest retailer is Mill Stores. There was previously a Wal-Mart located on the property, but it closed in 2005 and relocated to Colony Place, also in Plymouth.

The Hike

Start at Plymouth Rock heading north. Pass the Mayflower. Stay on sidewalks close to shore. Past the Plymouth fishing dock, boat launch, and stone jetty here is a more open area and then a Jordan Hospital site. If the tide is low climb down to the beach, where the sidewalk runs out and make your way to Nelson Park. If the tide is too high walk on north on Water Street to Nelson Park.

At Nelson Park go to the northwest corner. Here a bike trail starts and runs along the old railroad tracks. You can follow it all the way to the Cordage site or take small detours to the right down to the beach and back up to the trail or walk along the beach a ways and then make your way back up to the trail.

The trail ends at the currently used tracks for the commuter trains to Boston South Station. Just before the end, there is an open area where you can go over to the beach. You can also make a right at the end of the trail and go down Hedge Road and go down to the beach for a view.

From here, you retrace your steps back to your car.

Duxbury across the water

Plymouth North Beach

121

Plymouth Rock to Cordage Hike

3.   Morton Park Ponds

Directions and parking
From Plymouth's Main Street, turn west at Friendly's onto Summer Street. Cross over Rt. 3 and make the next left onto Morton Park Road. Follow into park and parking lot by public beach.
From Rt. 3 take Exit 6 west. By CVS make a left onto Pilgrim Hill Road and then a left onto Summer Street. Then make right onto Morton Park Road. Follow into park and parking lot by public beach.
Approximate GPS street address: Little Pond Rd., Plymouth, MA

Hike Difficulty
3.2 miles, 1:35 hours, some short hills

Features:
Billington Sea, Morton Park, Little Pond, pond beaches. Trail goes along shore of both ponds, great pond views.

Morton Park[4] is a park, located west of Route 3 and northwest of Lout Pond with its main entrance off Summer Street and its rear entrance off Billington Street. It is Plymouth's largest park area consisting of 200 acres (0.8 km²) of forest, the shoreline

122

of Little Pond, the northern shoreline of Billington Sea, the headwaters to Town Brook, and over two miles (3 km) of footpaths.

Billington Sea is a large shallow kettle pond situated on the westerly side of the town of Plymouth. It is located at 41' 56' 4" latitude, 70' 41" 16" longitude, at an elevation of 81' above sea level. It has a surface area of 269 acres, a shoreline of 7.3 miles, and median depths of from 7 to11feet, and is considered, by the state, to be a great kettle pond. A kettle pond is formed during the retreat of glaciers when large blocks of ice become buried in the outwash deposits and over eons of time the ice eventually melts leaving large depressions, which are referred to as kettles. The pond is recharged mostly by surface water from tributaries and groundwater sources. Studies show that the pond replaces itself every 55 days with over 400 million gallons of water.

The Hike
Start on the dirt road going east. Take a right at the triangle and then look for a trail on your left. It will take you to the shore of Billington Sea (BS). When you get to the T, there will be, on the left, a wooden bridge with a good view of Billington Sea. Go west or right from the T and follow the trail along the shore of BS. When you reach Hathaway Point, go north. The trail will take you to the dirt road. Go about ¼-mile. By-pass the first right and then make a right onto Little Pond Road (unmarked). Follow it about ½ miles to a road that angles south. There is a sign about Plymouth Beaches at the intersection. If you stay on Little Pond Road you will be back to the parking lot in about ½ mile. Alternatively, go south and follow the road around the southern end of Little Pond past where it makes a sweeping northeast turn. Then look for a small trail on the left heading towards Little Pond. This will take you to a trail that will take you around the shore of Little Pond back to the parking area. If you miss the trail, you can pick it up at the first beach area on the left.

Billington Sea

Little Pond   Lifeguard Stand

Morton Park Hike

4.   Plymouth Rock to Billington Sea (Pilgrim Trail)

Directions and parking
From Rt. 3 take Exit 6 towards Plymouth. Stay on Samoset Street, Cross Rt. 3A and continue to the rotary near the waterfront. Go right and park near Plymouth Rock. Approximate GPS street address: 45 Water St., Plymouth, MA

Hike Difficulty
4 miles, 1 hr. 45 min., slight uphill on the way out.

Features
Pilgrim Trail, Plymouth Rock, Brewster Gardens (Renovated 2006), Jenney Grist Mill, Jenny Pond Arm House Pond, Town Brook Reservoir, Billington Sea, Little Pond, and Covered wooden bridge.

Plymouth Rock[4]

Plymouth Rock is the traditional site of disembarkation of William Bradford and the *Mayflower* Pilgrims who founded Plymouth Colony in 1620, in what would become the United States. There is no contemporary reference to it, and it is not referred to in Bradford's journal *Of Plymouth Plantation* or in *Mourt's Relation*. The first reference to the Pilgrims landing on a rock is found 121 years after they landed. The rock is currently located on the shore of Plymouth Harbor in Plymouth, Massachusetts. Brewster Gardens[4] (aka Elder Brewster Gardens) is a park in Plymouth, located in the center of town. The park runs along both sides of Town Brook from the nature trail at the headwaters of the brook, past Jenney Grist Mill, underneath the Market Street and Main Street Extension (Route 3A) bridges to Water Street, across the street from the mouth of the brook, south of Plymouth Rock. Created in the early 1920's, the park covers the original garden plot that was granted to Elder William Brewster in 1620. Located in the park are a bronze statue, *The Pilgrim Maiden* by Henry Hudson Kitson (1922) and a stainless steel sculpture honoring Plymouth's immigrant settlers from 1700 to 2000.
Jenny Grist Mill, 6 Spring Lane (off Summer St., a short walk away from the waterfront), An authentic working mill rebuilt on the site of the original 1636 mill.

The Hike
The trail is marked with "Pilgrim Trail" markers. From Plymouth Rock go south, cross the street and enter Brewster Gardens. Cross the wooden bridge in Brewster Gardens, turn right, and follow the brook along its southern bank. At Jenney Pond cross over the pond and then once over the bridge go around the circle and take a trail on the western side up to Newfield Road. Cross it and continue along Town Brook Reservoir. Pass the covered wooden bridge, but do cross the next bridge over to Billington Road. Turn left and follow Billington Road under the underpass and into Morton Park. Follow the park road past a bog area and over a bridge. Shortly after the bridge turn left onto Little Pond Road. Keep a look out for a small trail going downhill from this dirt road towards Billington Sea. You will get to a T at Billington Sea. Turn left; go over wooden bridge with a great view of Billington Sea. Follow that trail back out to the road, turn right, and follow the road back till after the underpass. Now look for an old industrial building on the right. Turn half-right, pass by the building, and then turn left onto Off Billington Rd. The pond will be to your left. It feels like a private road here, but is not marked and the pond and the land around the northern end are Town of Plymouth property. Just past the pond cross the bridge to Billington Road and turn right. Follow it east about ¼ miles, then look for the wooden bridge on the right, and cross over. Then turn left and retrace your steps back to the car. Jenny Grist Mill can be a nice spot to enjoy an outdoor lunch in the summer.

Frank Werny

Billington Sea   Covered Bridge over brook

Swan Family on brook   Little Pond

Pilgrim Trail Hike

126

5.   Crawley Woodlands Preserve

Directions
From Exit 6 Rt. 3 go 0.3 mi east on Samoset St. Turn Right on OAK ST - go 0.4 mi
Turn Right on SUMMER ST. Bear Left on BILLINGTON ST - go 1.6 mi
Crawley Reserve sign will be obvious on the right.
Approximate GPS address across street from 330 Billington Street, Plymouth, MA

Features
Billington Sea, Lout Pond, Ponds, Lout Pond Rd, Branch Point Rd, dirt roads, wood
trail, bogs. The Crawleys Woodland Preserve is managed by the Town of Plymouth.
http://billingtonseapond.com/
Billington Sea (aka Billington's Sea) is a 269-acre (1.09 km^2) warm water pond
Morton Park lies on the pond's northern shore. The pond is fed by groundwater and
cranberry bog outlets. The average depth is seven feet and the maximum depth is
11 feet (3.4 m). The pond provides the headwaters to Town Brook. Seymour Island
is located in the center of the pond.
Billington Sea was named after Francis Billington, one of the passengers on the
Mayflower who sighted the pond from a tree in January 1621[1].
Lout Pond is an 18-acre (73,000 m^2) kettlehole pond, east of Billington Sea,
southeast of Morton Park, and northwest of Cooks Pond. The pond has an average
depth of 19 feet (5.8 m) and a maximum depth of 36 feet (11 m). The northern and
southern shores have been developed extensively. Cranberry bogs are along the
western shore, and Billington Street runs along the eastern shore. Due to the steep
bank only canoes and car top boats can be launched, electric motors only.

Difficulty
2.5 miles, 1:15 hrs, some short hills,

Hike
Go through the opening in the parking barrier. About half way along the hill on the
right the trail starts. The initial portion is well marked with square Town markers.
Follow the markers until your way is blocked by 3 stones. Turn right and again look
for the markers. They will stop and there should be red ribbons on the trees. Just
follow the trail towards Billington Sea. Once you see water, Billington Sea, follow
the meandering trail north. After crossing the bridge of the connector brook from
Lout Pond to Billington Sea, turn right. At the time of writing this the brook was
stagnant water. Follow the wide path down to the water. You will see the 3 stone
benches as you climb the stone steps. In the northeast corner of the cleared area you
can find a fairly obscure trail that will take you to the tip of the small peninsula. At
the tip turn back and look for another obscure trail to the left which takes you further
north along the water, but a few feet inland. Make your way through some small
trees that have invaded the trail till you come upon a wider trail taking you to the
right. Once you see the house on your left turn right onto Branch Point Road. After a
few feet take the trail to the left and follow it out to another portion of Lout Pond

Road. Once you pass the gate stay right. You will pass a canoe rental place on the left and then the road will take you out to Burgess Rd. Turn right and follow it out to Billington Road. Turn right again. After less than a quarter mile there will be a wooded hill on the right with a few mailboxes. This is Lout Pond road and will take you south When the road turns west, look for a dirt road to the left with 3 granite stones blocking the way. This is the continuation of Lout Road and will take you past Lout Pond and back to the car.

Billington Sea

Lout Pond

Memorial Benches

Crawley Woodlands Preserve Trail

6. Plymouth Long Beach
Directions and parking
From downtown Plymouth, take Rt. 3A south. After the bridge over Eel River, make a left into the Plymouth Long Beach parking lot.
From the north on Rt. 3 go south to exit 4. Follow to end and turn left onto Rt. 3A and then a right into the Plymouth Long Beach parking lot.
In the summer, there is a steep parking fee except for stickered vehicles. The rest of the year parking is free. Park near the north end of the lot.
Approximate GPS street address: Beach Park, Plymouth, MA

Hike Difficulty
6 miles on sandy and rocky road, soft and hard beach sand, about 2:15 hrs.

Features
Views of Plymouth Harbor, Cape Cod Bay, Saquish Head, Bug Light House, Clarks Island, and Gurnet Point. Beautiful beach on bay side, marshy beach on town side. Plymouth Beach 4, (also called Plymouth Long Beach or The Point) is a small village located in Plymouth, Massachusetts, United States. It is located directly south of Plymouth Center, and is adjacent to Plimoth Plantation. Plymouth Beach consists of a motel, a restaurant and a small beachside community along Warren Cove. The village [4] is best known for its prominent barrier beach. The beach is approximately three miles in length. It begins just south of the Eel River bridge on Route 3A, and juts out almost due north, running along the last ½ mile (0.8 km) of the river before it empties into Plymouth Harbor. The barrier beach offers protection for Plymouth Harbor.

Plymouth Beach is also an important breeding and nesting site for several threatened and endangered shorebirds, including the Piping Plover and the Least, Arctic, Common and Roseate Terns. The barrier beach serves as a critical migratory stopover site. Over 20,000 migratory shorebirds use Plymouth Beach as a "fuel stop" to put on weight before continuing long distance migration. The birds' routes typically span up to 3,000 miles (4,858 km) of non-stop flight. The most northerly 3,000 feet (914 m) of the barrier beach has been protected and maintained as a tern and piping plover colony by the Massachusetts Audubon Society, and is owned by the Town of Plymouth.

Bug Light[4] also called Duxbury Pier Light
Height: 47 feet, 35 feet above water. Construction: cast iron
Color: Red Characteristics: Group red flashing 2 times every 10 seconds
Range: 6 nautical miles Fog signal: one blast each 15 seconds

History
Duxbury Pier Light was built in 1871 on the north side of the main channel in Plymouth Harbor to mark the dangerous shoal off Saquish Head. The unusual coffeepot-shaped lighthouse is locally known as "Bug Light" or simply "The Bug." The lighthouse contains three levels that were used as living quarters and a watch room. The lantern room held a fourth order Fresnel lens, first lighted on September 15, 1871. To protect the structure, 100 tons of stones were placed around the base in 1886. A 700-gallon water cistern was added in 1900. The lighthouse was automated in 1964 and the keepers were removed. A modern optic replaced the Fresnel lens. Over the next two decades Duxbury Pier Light fell victim to much vandalism and seabirds made themselves a home in the interior. Bug Light survived the Hurricane of 1944 when 30-foot waves battered the isolated station. Heavy seas on the east side destroyed the fog bell mechanism, the light keepers' boat, and its outhouse. In 1983 Duxbury Pier Light was slated by the Coast Guard to be replaced by a fiberglass tower much like the one that had replaced Boston Harbor's old Deer Island Lighthouse. The Coast Guard had estimated that a renovation of the current structure would have cost $250,000. A group of concerned local residents formed Project Bug Light. A five-year lease was granted to the preservation committee. The Coast Guard sandblasted and painted the structure and did some repair work in 1983; the work was completed in 1985. The Coast Guard spent $100,000 to refurbish the lower half of the lighthouse. Project Bug Light raised $20,000 from local businesses, as well as sales of T-shirts and bumper stickers, a fashion show, baseball games, and raffling a painting. They used this money to restore the upper parts and the interior, including the rebuilding of the roof and the catwalk. At the same time, solar power replaced the older battery system. The fog signal was also converted to solar power. In the late 1980s, vandals broke into the lantern room, leaving it susceptible to leaks. The weather deteriorated the wood interior so much that all the wood had to be removed, leaving bare iron walls. After a few years, Project Bug Light virtually dissolved as an organization, and the five-year lease expired. In 1993, the Coast Guard again talked of replacing the lighthouse with a fiberglass pole, or at least removing the lantern room. This time, Dr. Don Muirhead of Duxbury, an avid sailor, spearheaded a new

preservation effort. The Coast Guard again refurbished the lighthouse in 1996. The volunteers of Project Bug Light continue to do maintenance at the light and have raised more than $80,000 toward the continued preservation of "The Bug." To quote volunteer Edwin Heap, "It's an ugly old historical thing, but we're glad it's been saved."

Clark's Island4 is the name of a small island located in Plymouth in the U.S. state of Massachusetts. It was named for the first mate of the *Mayflower*, the ship that brought the Pilgrims to New England. The island was initially considered for the location of the Pilgrim's settlement, but was rejected in favor of a site to the south, which became known as Massachusetts. Today Clark's Island is a part of the town of Plymouth.

While it is rumored that Truman Capote wrote much of *In Cold Blood* while staying at a cottage on the island, he actually wrote the novella *Breakfast at Tiffany's* there.

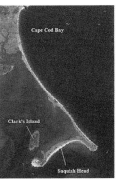

Clark's Island is located in Plymouth, a part of Plymouth Bay. Although physically closer to the town of Duxbury, the island is officially part of the town of Plymouth, as are the outermost points of Duxbury Beach, Saquish Neck, and Gurnet Point. The island is located north of the Duxbury Pier Light and Saquish Neck, and west of Saquish Head.

The Hike
Ideally this hike is done near low tide. If the tide is sufficiently out climb over the rock wall at the north end of the parking lot and head north on the beach.
If the tide is too high start on the dirt road by the guard shack and stay on it till you can cross over and proceed north without getting wet. After the first 2 miles, the beach will expand to 100 yards wide when the tide is out. Either way you get great views of Cape Cod Bay, Gurnet Point, Clarks Island, and Bug Light House on the right and dunes on the left as you approach the tip. Follow the tip around to the left and return on the town side of the peninsula. There are great marshy areas and a view of Plymouth. As you run out of beach to walk on, going south, the road will be to your left and it will take you back to the parking lot.

Bug Light House   Plymouth Long Beach

131

Blowing sands   Crossing over

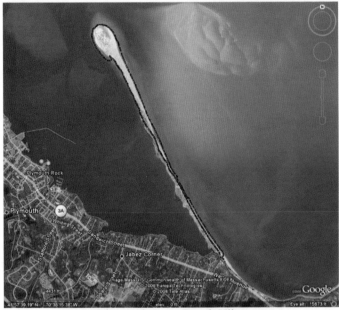

Plymouth Long Beach Hike

Beach Plums

7.   Town Forest; Cooks Pond

Directions and parking
From Rt. 3 Exit 5 take Long Pond Road south for about a mile. After you pass the Middle School entrances on the left there will be a Town Forest sign on the left just before Drew Road. Park somewhere here.
Approximate GPS address: 127-8 Long Pond Rd., Plymouth, MA

Hike Difficulty
3.5 miles, 1:20 hours, some short hills, some bushwhacking.

Features
Cooks Pond, pine forest, active cranberry bogs, Town Forest.
Cooks Pond[4] is a 23-acre reservoir within the Eel River watershed, located north of South Pond village, near *The Shops at 5* and the main Post Office, and southeast of Lout Pond. The pond suffers from trash along the northern shore as well as erosion at the access point on the north side of the pond, each of which was noted in a 2002 field inspection.

The Hike
From the Parking lot, take the trail west, but not Drew Road, which is going southwest. Follow the trail down to where it meets Town Forest Road coming from the power lines. Turn right and go north for a little over ¼ mile. Look for a way down to Cooks Pond. When you reach Cooks Pond, find open areas just up from the shore, and work your way to the southern tip of the pond. Now you will briefly be on private property. You will see a small bog area. Make your way down to it and walk around to the right keeping the pond on your right. Pass below the house along the pond. Just beyond the house, find a trail going to the left and up. You are now continuing on Dept of Fish and Game Land. Follow it all the way to a large bog area owned by Kapell Pinnacle Watercourse Trust. Make your way across the bogs to Watercourse Road. Now turn around and start your way back along the north side of the bogs. This is Cooke's Point Road. When you get to the two small ponds, make a left turn after the smaller one and before the larger one. This is still Cooke's Point Road. Stay on it until you see some buildings on the left. Now you are near the schools. Follow the outer perimeter of the school south and then a trail just off Long Pond Road back to the car.

Bog Ponds

Snow Covered Bogs

133

Town Forest Hike

8.   Town Forest; South Triangle Pond

Directions and parking
From Rt. 3 Exit 5 take Long Pond Road west, turning south. After passing the commercial area and then the school entrances on the right, there will be signage about the Town Forest. Turn right onto Drew Road (dirt). After passing South Triangle Road you will see South Triangle Pond on the right and a parking area where the trail to the pond starts.
Approximate GPS address: 77 Drew Road, Plymouth, MA

Hike Difficulty
About 2.5 miles; 1 ½ hours; There are some short hills along the way

Features
This is a quiet walk through the woods touching on South Triangle Pond, Great South Pond and the Jenkins Hole.
South Triangle Pond[4] is a 15-acre (61,000 m^2) within the Eel River watershed. The pond is located north of South Pond village in the Plymouth Town Forest, east of Great South Pond and south of Plymouth's main Post Office and *The Shops at 5*.
Great South Pond is a 292-acre (1.2 km^2) reservoir within the Eel River watershed, located southeast of Little South Pond, west of South Triangle Pond, and north of

Boot Pond. The pond serves as a secondary municipal water supply for the Town of Plymouth.

The Hike
Start by walking down to the pond to the west for a view of the pond and then back up. Cross the street, enter the woods were you see the Wildlands Trust trail marker. After about 30 feet make a left and follow the trail markers for about 100 feet north. This part of the trail is not well worn. It is marked by Wildlands Trust trail markers. Then make a right following the trail markers. After about 500 feet there will be a T with another trail. Turn left and follow the markers for a while then make a right, again following the markers. This will take you to near Jenkins Hole. Jenkins Hole will be down the hill to your left. You can venture off the trail down to the water. Return to the trail up the slope and follow it west. This will take you back to the north-south trail. Turn right or south and follow it south for about 1 mile or 15 plus minutes. You will cross a dirt road, Fuller Farm Rd. Continue straight across following the trail markers. When you reach a high point from which you can see Great South Pond you have reached the end of the trail and should turn around and retrace your steps back to the car. It is possible to make your way down to the road along the pond, but it is private. At the pond turn right and follow the private road along the shoreline till the road turns east away from the pond. Follow the road and make your way back to Drew Road. Turn right and go about ¾ miles back to the car.

Great South Pond   Jenkins Hole

South Triangle Pond Trail

VII.   North of Plymouth: Duxbury Pembroke Kingston

1. **Bay Farm and Mulliken's Landing**
2. **Camp Wing**
3. **Duxbury Beach**
4. **Duxbury Bogs**
5. **Lansing Bennett Forest**
6. **North Hill Marsh**
7. **Round Pond**
8. **Steward Preserve**
9. **Tucker Preserve**
10. **Willow Brook**

Distribution of Hikes North of Plymouth

1.   **Bay Farm and Mulliken's Landing**

Directions
Take Rt. 3 to Exit 9. Turn right off ramp. Turn right onto Landings Road.
Mullikan's Landing will be on right after you pass under Rt. 3.
Park there.
Approximate GPS address 64 Landing Rd, Kingston, MA

Features
Mulliken's Landing; Bay Farm; Kingston Bay; meadows; rock outcroppings along
the beach.

Mulliken's Landing
The Town of Kingston now has canoe/kayak car-top access on the estuary of the
Jones River at the former LaPlante property. Dedicated as Mulliken's Landing at the
AhDeNah during Kingston's first Earth Walk 2002 event, this newly acquired 2.36-
acre parcel is now open to the public. Acquisition of the property could not have
been achieved without the diligence of all partners, in particular the Jones River
Watershed Association, the Town of Kingston, and programs and offices of the
Executive Office of Energy and Environmental Affairs. http://www.mass.gov
BayFarm:
http://www.town.duxbury.ma.us/public_documents/DuxburyMA_Conservation/Con
Areas/bayfarm

Difficulty
2.9 miles, 1:20 hrs, very flat, some rock outcroppings along the beach

Hike
Start in the southwest corner of the Mulliken's landing and walk through the reeds to
Jones River. Return to parking area, turn right and follow River Street all the way to
Jones River. Admire the view and then turn around and make your first right onto
Bayside Lane. Near the end of bayside lane there is a circle and a sign at about 1
o'clock directing you to the Bay Farm Reservation trail. When you reach the yellow
trail junction take a right and follow to the orange trail to the right. This will lead to
the bay. Follow the trail and stay right, which will take you north along the bay.
When you can make a right the trail will take you to a rock outcropping on the
beach. From the rocks make your way back to the trail and then still stay to your
right. This will bring you to the beach again and the southern terminus of the Bay
Circuit Trail. Turn around and follow the trail to the right. It will circle around along
the perimeter of the meadow till you get to the Bay Farm parking area. You can now
go left on the street and till you get back to the Mulliken's Landing parking area, or,
make a left into the meadow and go to just after the first boardwalk and a trail to
your right. At the junction make a left and go till you meet up with the orange trail
and turn right. This will take you to the trail to Bayside Lane and then out to River
Street. Turn right and walk back to the parking lot at Mulliken's Landing.

Mulliken's Landing

Bay Farm Beach

North River

Myles Standish Monument

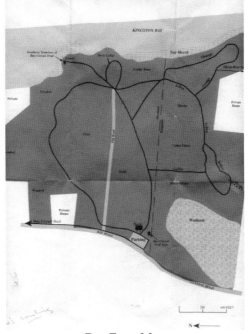

Bay Farm Map

Mulliken's Landing, Bay Farm Hike

2. Camp Wing Conservation Area

Directions
Take Rt.3 Exit 11. Turn west off ramp. Follow Congress Street past Sun Tavern (12.1 miles) and turn sharp right onto Franklin Street. Circular drive and signage will be on left (0.4 miles).
Approximate GPS address 660 Franklin Street, Duxbury, MA 02332

Features
Quiet walk in the pines; Fen and Marsh overlook; South River, Camp Wing Conservation Area

Camp Wing Conservation Area
http://www.town.duxbury.ma.us/Public_Documents/DuxburyMA_Conservation /ConAreas/campwing
Camp Wing Conservation Area is unique because there is almost no human impact. This makes the large parcel excellent for animals that need to be far from human activities. Camp Wing contains these five natural communities which taken together, support an exceptional diversity of plants and rare animals.
Open Water: The shallow segment of the South River serves as high quality habitat for water fowl such as Great Blue Herons, mallards and other migratory water fowl,

as well as raccoons, opossum and even otters. Common plant species include Big Duckweed, Common Bladderwort, and Wool Grass

Marsh: On this area of low-lying waterlogged land grows emergent vegetation like Wide-leafed Cattail and Blue Joint. It is difficult to cross on foot due to soft, wet ground.

Shrub Swamp: The shrub wetlands, near the abandoned cranberry bog, are probably the result of forest cutting 40-50 yrs ago. This may very gradually become forested again. Common plant species include Red Maple, Sweet Pepperbush, and Green Briar.

Fen: The grasses, sedges, and sphagnum moss of this low, nutrient-poor marshy area is located on the northern half of the abandoned cranberry bog.

Upland forest: The transition from Camp Wing s wetlands to upland invites a variety of plants found in both wetlands and upland. The timber harvest in the past promoted native tree species such as Red Maple, Eastern White Pine, and both White and Red Oak. You will notice that the trees are much younger and smaller as they are in the process of reforestation.

Actual Camp Wing is located at 742 Keene St. in Duxbury

Difficulty
None; Clearly marked trails, 1.7 miles; 45 minutes

Hike
From the parking lot take the 'Blue' trail. At the orange trail turn left. Then turn left onto the 'Green' trail. Cross a boardwalk and then look for the red trail to the left. Follow the red trail to a junction that to the left will take you to an observation platform over Fen Swamp. Here the trail is marked closed. If it is not you can continue to where South river flows from Fen Marsh into Red Maple Swamp. To return turn left at the 'Red' trail, then left at the 'Green' trail and left again at the orange trail and the ' Blue' which will take you back to the parking lot.

Board Walk

Bright Green Moss

141

Fen   Orchis and Ground Pine (club moss)

Camp Wing Trails

142

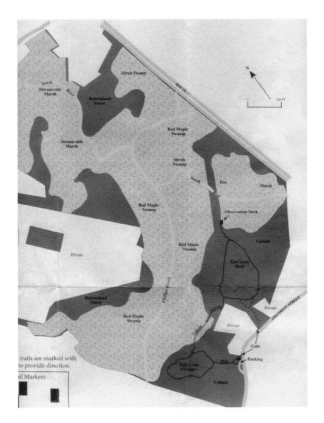

3.   **Duxbury Beach**

Directions and parking to Powder Point Bridge and Duxbury Beach
Take Rt. 3 Exit 10 East Tremont Street, Duxbury going toward Chestnut Street.
Turn right on Alden Street go 0.6 mi.
Turn right on St. George Street, go 0.5 mi
Turn left on Washington Street, go < 0.1 mi
Continue on Powder Point Ave., go 1.1 mi
Bear left on Powder Point Bridge Rd, 1 mi
Arrive at Powder Point Bridge, Duxbury
In the summer there is very limited parking on the west end of the bridge. Rest of
year cars may cross the bridge and park by the east end.
Approximate GPS street address: Powder Point Bridge, Duxbury, MA

Hike Difficulty
8-miles to Plymouth Lighthouse out and back, 2.5 hours; 14 miles to Saquish Head
out and back, 4 hours; flat; hard sand on beach; soft sand on road.

Features:
Plymouth Light House, Gurnet Point, Saquish Beach; Saquish Head, great beach on east side, beautiful marshes and bay on west side; Former site of Fort Standish. Duxbury Beach is four miles long and is accessed by the Powder Point Bridge from Duxbury.
It is a barrier beach, defined by sand dunes, Rosa Ragusa, and beach grass. It is 50 yards wide at some points, and is the sole land access to the villages of Saquish and Gurnet Point across the town line in Plymouth, the only land area where the two towns meet. The northern residential end is protected by an Army Corps Of Engineers concrete seawall.
One of the first trans-Atlantic cables came ashore here at Rouse's Hummock, and the first call was made on it (to President James Garfield) by Napoleon III.
It is the home of the former Gurnet Classic Beach Run.
Piping plovers nest there, protected by the town's conservation officers. There is a town beach and a public beach. The north end is developed, while the southern end is marred only by an access road.
Duxbury Beach suffers terribly in hurricanes and nor'easters. It is widely considered the focal point of damages in both The Blizzard of '78 and The Perfect Storm of 1991.
Gurnet Point4 , also known as The Gurnet, is located at the end of the Duxbury Beach peninsula at the entrance to Plymouth in Plymouth, Massachusetts, and is a headland and the small private settlement located on it. The Pilgrims who settled Plymouth in 1620 named it Gurnett's Nose for its resemblance to headlands in the English Channel where *gurnett* fish were plentiful. The Gurnet (pronounced *gurn-it* with the accent on the first syllable) is the home of Plymouth (Gurnet) Lighthouse as well as of Fort Andrews from the Revolutionary War. Its only access by land is from the Powder Point Bridge at Duxbury Beach 5 miles to the north by foot or by 4-wheel drive beach buggies, but access is restricted to property owners, residents and their guests, except for once a year on Memorial Day when the lighthouse is open to the public.

The Hike
Pick a time when the tide is low and start the hike on the beach. Go south for about 4 miles on the beach till you get to the wooden stairs up to the small beach community on Gurnet Point. Turn left up their main road. Take your third right and find the trail up to the Plymouth Lighthouse. It is actually in Duxbury, but Saquish is in Plymouth. The view of Plymouth bay from here is great.
Now you can turn around and return by way of the main road all the way back to the parking lot with beautiful marshes and Duxbury Bay on your left.
Alternatively, you can turn around and stay to your left, which will take you to Saquish. You can than walk an additional 3 miles along the beach to Saquish Head and pass the former site of Fort Standish. From where the beach turns very rocky, you have a 7-mile trip back. First, you must return to Gurnet Point. There is no shortcut across the marsh. Then you can return from there via the western side along Duxbury Bay.

144

Beach Cottages on Saquish Neck   Powder Point Bridge

Gurnet Point   Plymouth Lighthouse

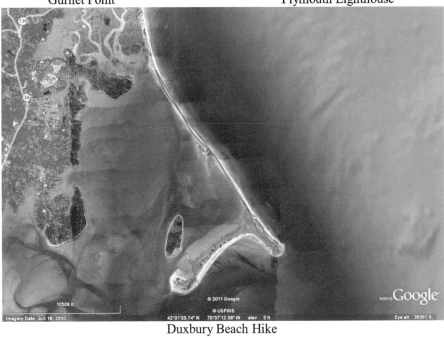

Duxbury Beach Hike

4. Duxbury Bogs

Directions
Take Hwy 3 to exit 9. Take 3A west to Hwy 53. Turn right onto Hwy 53. Go a little over 1 mile. Turn right onto Winter Street. Turn left onto Elm Street. Shortly turn right onto East Street. Park on left off East Street just before Hwy 3.
Or
From Rt. 3 South: Take Exit 10 off Rt. 3 Follow Rt. 3A east to the Duxbury Fire Station. Turn left onto and continue down Mayflower Street. At the end of Mayflower Street, take a sharp left onto East Street. Follow East Street just over Rt. 3 and parking will be on your right.
Approximate GPS address: 200 East St., Duxbury, MA

Hike Difficulty
Total distance 2.3 miles. 1 hr., flat except for a very minor hill.

Features
The hike circles three good size bogs in the area, including Lovings and Lorings Bogs, and touches on two ponds. In addition, you will pass through a beautiful stand of large pines.

Hike
From the parking area stay to your right and follow the trail north along the water passing Lovings Bog on your left and then Lorings Bog, also on your left, t ill you get into a wooded area. Follow the trail into the wooded area, go up and then down the little hill. Turn right at the bottom of the hill onto a narrower trail between two small bodies of water. Follow this till you get to the road. Go left onto the road to the shed and return on the other side of the small bog now going south. You will emerge by Lovings Bog. By the bog on the left make a left and go north along the bog till you get to Cranberry Factory Pond. Turn south and follow the bog till you come out by Lovings Bog. Turn south again heading back to the parking area.

Pump house by bog

Wintery Bog

Ducks and Geese on Lovings Boggs

Duxbury Bog Hike

5. Lansing-Bennett Forest

Directions and parking
Take Rt. 3 to exit 11. Go west on Rt. 14. (~1/2 mile)
Turn left onto King Phillips Path. Go ~ ¾ mile. Right onto Union Bridge Rd.
Parking on left.
Approximate GPS street address: 300 Union Bridge Rd., Duxbury, MA

Hike Difficulty
About 2.4 miles, 1 hr., flat

Features
Phillips Mill Pond, Upper Chandler Pond, Phillips Brook, Marked trails, Thadeus
Chandler Sanctuary, Black Friars Swamp, Lansing Bennett Forest

Lansing Bennett Forest[4]
The town conservation area formerly known as Trout Farm was dedicated in 2005 to
the memory of Dr. Lansing Bennett, chair of the Duxbury Conservation Commission
from 1967 to 1979. Dr. Lansing Bennett sought to preserve the rural charm of
Duxbury and its wetland resources by developing the greenbelt plan of land
extending along the river watershed throughout the town. During his time on the
Commission, he helped obtain more than 1,200 acres of conservation land within the
greenbelt and secured the passage of the Wetlands and Watershed Protection District
Bylaw. The 344 acres that comprise the Lansing Bennett Forest was one of his most
satisfying acquisitions. The renaming of this parcel is a fitting tribute to a dedicated
public servant.
Lansing Bennett Forest was purchased by the Town in July of 1970 from the Lot
Philips Company, a wooden box manufacturer formerly located in Hanover. This
large parcel made up of three contiguous lots to form one large wooded lot of mixed
upland and wetland. The Phillips Brook watershed occupies about 25 to 30 percent
of the parcel of the land and is maple swamp considered wetlands. The remainder of

148

the parcel is a largely pine-oak mixed forest. The terrain is made up of kettle holes, the pits or depressions left by the melting of isolated blocks of ice, leaving several hills and valleys with some steep-sided hills. It appears that today's topography is just as the glaciers left it upon retreating many thousand years ago. There are several hiking trails throughout the property, including a portion of the Bay Circuit Trail, which runs through from Union Bridge Road to Summer St. on its way across Duxbury.

The Last Mill in Duxbury

Built circa 1830, Howland's Mill was probably the last mill built in Duxbury. It was situated on the east bank of Phillips Brook, southeast of Franklin and Union Street. These two streets were old Native American trails, turned later into cart paths, that allowed access to the Mill. It was originally built as a gristmill but was later changed to a sawmill. This mill had many problems with too little water. A ditch was dug through a hill bringing water out of Black Friars Swamp across Franklin Street to the stream. This ditch can still be seen alongside the bank of the brook. The old mill foundation can also still be seen. The granite foundation sides still hold. The mill faced Franklin Street and had a large wheel several feet below the dam. Water was funneled over the dam and dropped on the wheel to power the mill. From there, the water ran under the street through a culvert.

Vegetation and Wildlife

The vegetation along Phillips Brook is characteristic of wetlands habitat. The understory along the edge is made up of sweet pepperbush and high-bush blueberry. The primary species tree is the red maple constituting a typical maple swamp. The upland areas are a pine-oak mix, the primary trees being eastern white pine, red oak, and white oak. In some spots, there is a small population of eastern hemlock. In the pine-oak upland forest, there is very little understory vegetation. Some of the kettle holes have typical maple swamp vegetation and some standing water in them. In both the uplands and along the brook there is poison ivy, so please be careful. The Lansing Bennett Forest uplands mixed with wetlands provide a diverse habitat for a wide range of inhabitants. Small mammals include mice, chipmunks, both red and grey squirrels, opossum, raccoon, and possibly otter. The only large mammals that inhabit these woods are white-tailed deer. In the wetlands, the reptiles and amphibians dominate. There are painted, spotted, and box turtles in both the wooded and brook front areas. There are a number of salamanders and frogs living under rocks and logs along the brook. The most common are the red back salamander, wood frog, and the American toad. There are a fair number of woodland bird species such as black-capped chickadee, white-throated sparrow, blue jay and an occasional woodpecker, red-tailed hawk, and great horned owl. However, these are not the only species that inhabit these woods. The trout in Phillips Brook are what give this conservation land its name.

The Trout of Lansing Bennett Forest
Flowing south to north, Phillips Brook is a 1.8-mile long tributary of the South River. This brook was known to contain trout. After the Howland's sawmill closed, Phillips Brook was used as a trout farm. The fish were transported by train to the markets and restaurants in Boston. The upper section, above Union Bridge Road was the site of the farm. Evidence of fish ladders once developed here, can be seen at the edge of the stream. Trout prefer areas in which they can hide such as deep pools, whirlpools, and the covered edges of stream banks. The brook continues to contain good wild brook and brown trout populations. A study by the Division of Fisheries and Wildlife (DFW) was done in 1997 to determine the health of the trout population. DFW discovered both adult and juvenile brook and brown trout indicating that the brook contained reproducing wild populations of brook and brown trout.

The Charcoal Pit
Along the trail, leading from the parking area is a former charcoal pit. After the American Revolution, the ship building industry required charcoal for the smelting of bog iron ore. Trees were cut and piled in a circle twenty feet in diameter and dirt was piled over this pyramid after the fire was established. After several days, the dirt was pulled off and the charcoal removed. The process created a circular mound containing the charcoal, which is still visible more than 100 years later.

The Hike

From the parking area take the yellow trail till you get to the red trail. Turn left and then at the white trail turn left again and stay on it till you get to Summer Street. Be careful crossing Summer Street. On the other side slightly to the left is another trail that will take you through the Thaddeus Chandler Sanctuary to Upper Chandler Pond. Admire the pond and then make your way back along the same trail. After you cross the road, again follow the white trail. Pass up the black and red trails. The white trail will cross Phillips brook on a bridge, then take you through Black Friars Marsh on a boardwalk, and then past Howland's Mill site. when you reach the yellow trail, make a left, and follow it back to the parking lot.

Lansing Bennett Forest Hike

6. North Hill Marsh Conservation Area

Directions and parking
From Rt. 3 South: Take Exit 10 off Rt. 3 and bear to the right. Follow Rt. 3A to the Duxbury Fire Station. Turn left onto and continue down Mayflower Street. Parking for North Hill Marsh Conservation Area is about a mile past the Duxbury transfer station on the right.
Approximate GPS street address 500 Mayflower St., Duxbury, MA

Hike Difficulty
3.1 miles, 1:20 hrs. some narrow trails, some short steep portions. Well marked trails.

Features
North Hill Pond, North Hill Marsh, Audubon Wildlife Sanctuary, Great walk along the shore of the North Hill Pond. North Hill Marsh Pond[4] is a 38-acre pond in Duxbury, USA. The pond is the headwaters to the Back River. The pond is located northeast of Round Pond and north of Island Creek Pond. A wildlife sanctuary borders this pond to the south, and the North Hill Country Club, accessible via Merry Avenue, off Route 14, borders this pond to the northeast. The water quality is impaired due to non-native aquatic plants in the pond.

The Hike
From the parking lot, take the yellow trail off to the left. Stay to your right and follow it straight down to the platform overlooking the pond. Just past the platform is a trail to the right again that will lead to the blue trail, which is marked all the way around the pond. After a little over ¼ mile, the trail comes to a junction> Male a sharp cutback down the hill and follow the blue markers. The trail now follows the shoreline, but, sometimes over 100 yards from it. After about 1 mile, the trail goes between the golf course and the pond. Stay just to the left of the golf course and then go left and cross the pond dam. After the dam make a left and then a right at the T. the shortly look for the blue trail to the left. The continuation of the trail is marked by two boulders. Again, follow the blue markers. The trail becomes smaller and more obscure. Stay to the left and it will bring you to the platform where it first started. Take a right by the viewing platform and follow the yellow trail back to the parking lot.

Autumn Scene on Pond   Lone Swan on Pond

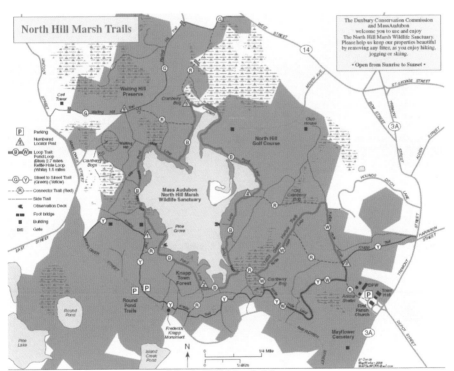

North Hill Marsh Map

153

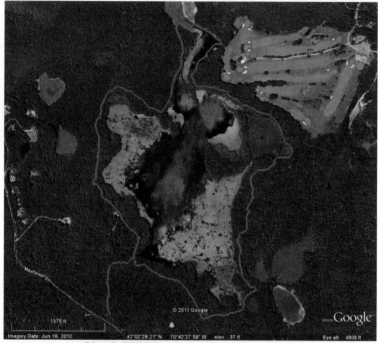

North Hill Marsh Conservation Trail

7.   Round Pond Conservation Area

Directions
From Rt. 3 South: Take Exit 10 off Rt. 3 and bear to the right. Follow Rt. 3A east to the Duxbury Fire Station. Turn left onto and continue down Mayflower Street. Parking for Round Pond and North Marsh areas is about a mile past the Duxbury transfer station on the left. Park in North Marsh parking area, which comes first. Approximate GPS street address: 500 Mayflower St., Duxbury, MA

Difficulty:
3.4 miles, 1:30 hrs. some slight hills, rest flat.

Features:
Bogs; Ponds; Round Pond; Island Creek Pond; Pine Lake; Chase Reservoir.
Island Creek Pond[4] is a 43-acre pond in the village of Tinkertown is located north of Mill Pond, south of North Hill Marsh, and southwest of Pine Lake and Round Pond. The pond is the headwaters to Island Creek. The water quality is impaired due to non-native aquatic plants and non-native fish in the pond. Crocker Park, an open space area owned by the Town of Duxbury, is situated along the southern shore of the pond.

154

Pine Lake[4] is a 23-acre (93,000 m^2) lake in the village of Tinkertown. The lake is located southwest of Round Pond, northwest of Island Creek Pond, and east of Route 3 near the East Street underpass. The outflow is a small stream that flows into Round Pond. A small subdivision lies along the southern shore of the lake.

The Hike
From North Marsh parking area head cross the street and go back a few feet till you get to the beginning of the red trail. Follow the red trail staying right to the T. Go left. After a few feet make another left, which will take you along, island Creek Pond. It is a minor trail. After a couple of hundred yards, there will be a noticeable trail to the right. Take it to the red trail and turn left. When you reach a sand/dirt area turn left again and follow the trail to the pump house on Island Creek Pond and around the bogs back to the red trail. Turn left on the red trail and then right onto the white trail just before the next bog and pond. Follow the white trail past Deer Lake and then turn left when you can, and follow the shoreline to Chase reservoir. Stay east of the reservoir. Make a right when you can and go between the bogs to Round Pond and the pump house. Follow the white trail around the pond to the left. As the white trail leaves the pond area, take the yellow trail to the right. It will bring you back to the road. Just before the road take a small trail to the right and it will take you back to the North Marsh parking area.

Trail Head

White Trail

Chase Reservoir

Round Pond

155

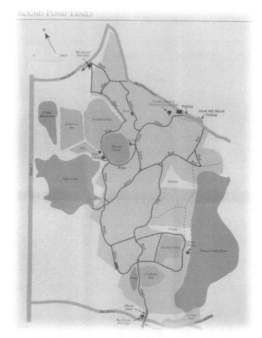

Round Pond Conservation Area Map

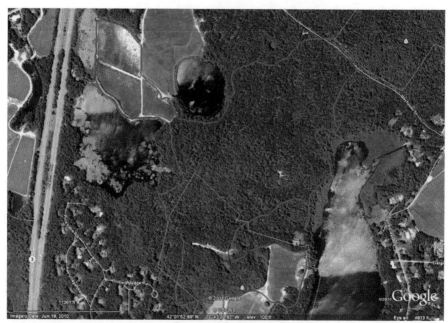

Round Pond Trail

156

8. O. W. Steward Preserve

Directions and parking
Rt. 3 to Exit 9.Go on north Rt. 3A about ½ miles. Turn left onto Rt. 80.
At stop sign, turn left and continue on Rt. 80. Pass Indian Pond Rd.
And, about 3 miles from Rt. 3, turn left onto Sylvia Place Rd.
Parking lot is on right just past Bryant Mill Pond.
Approximate GPS street address: Sylvia Place Rd., Kingston, MA

Hike Difficulty
2.5 miles, 1 hr, some short steep hills, minor bushwhacking

Features:
Bryant Mill Pond, Sylvia Place Pond, Russell Pond, fish ladder and brook connecting
ponds.
In 1856, Sylvanus Bryant Jr. and Noah Prince set up a sawmill to make boards for
boxes. By 1879, Bryant had bought out Prince; he continued to operate the mill until
1900.

Bryant's Pond, 1925, by Emily Fuller Drew
This view, taken from the O.W. Stewart Preserve (part of the Wildlands Trust of
Southeastern Massachusetts), shows some of the buildings around Bryant's Pond. In
the left foreground stands a small boathouse, and behind it to the right is the Bryant
Boxboard Mill. Behind the mill, the Lyman-John Cushman house and barn can be
seen, along with a dirt road that is today's Sylvia's Place Road. At the far left is the
Deacon Cushman House, which today is 33 Indian Pond Road.
Source: Life on the River by Carrie Elliott, 2005

The Hike
The trail starts right from the parking area just beyond Bryant Mill Pond. Follow the
Wildlands Trust trail t Sylvia Place Pond. There turn left. At the wooden board
bridge, cross over and take the small trail up the hill on the left rather than going

around Sylvia Place Pond. At the top of the short hill, turn right. Follow that trail to the first trail to the left or southeast. That trail although partly overgrown will follow the ridge along the west shore of Russell Pond. When you start seeing a sand or bog area on your right find a way down. There is no trail. Once on the low flat area follow it around to the northeast corner. Reenter the woods and bushwhack northwest up the hill till you run across a trail going north or northeast. This will take you back to short steep trail down to the wooden board bridge. Turn left or west before crossing the bridge and follow the shore of Sylvia Place Pond. At the southern tip the trail will cross a small bridge made of rotting sticks. It can be slippery! Follow the trail north over a fish ladder and between Bryant Mill and Sylvia Place Ponds all the way back to the car. Alternatively, follow the trail north about 100 yards and look for a Wildlands Trust trail sign on the left. Enter the woods there and follow the trail markers, some Wildlands Trust, and some blue dot. If you lose them head up hill till you see a bog area below and then turn right and follow the ridge till you find trail marker or see Rt. 80. When you get close to the triangle formed by Sylvia Place road and Rt. 80, you should still see the markers. Follow them downhill to the right till you reach the trail along the west side of Bryant Mill Pond. Turn right; follow the trail to the bottom of the fish ladder. Walk up to the top, turn left and follow the trail between Bryant Mill and Sylvia Place Ponds and stay left all the way back to the car.

Fish ladder

Sylvia Place Pond

Board Bridge

Bryant Mill Pond

O. W. Steward Preserve Trail

Reflections!

9.   Tucker Preserve and Luddam's Ford
There are two hikes here 9a. Tucker Preserve is out and back on the southeast side of Indian Head River all in the woods and 9b. Luddam's Ford and Tucker Preserve, which goes out on one side and back on the other. It does follow a few feet of road along the way.

9a.   Tucker Preserve

Directions and parking
Rt. 3 to exit 12 West on Rt. 139 to Rt. 53 south. After ~ 1 mile, turn right at the light onto Rt. 14. After 1 ½ miles turn right onto Oldham Street After ¾ mile right onto W. Elm. Go 2 miles to Town Park and dam on right. Park just past the dam.
Approximate GPS address: 490 West Elm Street, Pembroke, MA

Hike Difficulty
3.9 miles 1.5 hours, rocky brook crossing, some short hills on trail.

Features
Indian Head River, Curtis Crossing Dam, rocky gorge, small brook, quiet walk in the woods, scenic river views.
The Indian Head River[4] is located on the Hanover, Pembroke border and covers about 8 acres (32,000 m^2). It was probably a fishing and travel spot for Wompatuck Indians. The river runs through the Luddams Ford Park named after a guide, James Luddam, who carried Governor Winthrop across the river to get to Weymouth, Massachusetts. In November 1873, Eugene H. Clapp bought the Old Forge Property from George Curtis and built the Clapp Rubber Factory on the river. The factory is no longer there, but the mercury pollution from the factory still clings to the rocks and fish making it unsafe to drink the water and eat the fish. There is a strip of rubber along the river on the Pembroke side which people may bounce on.
The river now has a manmade dam and fish ladder. The river is stocked with trout. It also has a small beaver population. For two weeks during the summer, the herring run upstream to spawn.

The Hike
The initial portion is clearly marked with Wildlands Trust markers. Start near the river heading west. Follow the trail staying to the right a few feet from the water. Continue following the trail and admire the view on the right. Eventually you get to a small tributary or brook and must turn left. Make your way up the brook. The trail is not that clearly marked here. You will reach a place where there is an obvious rocky crossing over the brook. After you cross, stay right. When you reach the dirt road, go right, and stay right. This will take you down to the river. At the river, you can turn right or downstream and go till you reach a scenic small waterfall. At this point, you turn around and retrace your steps. Stay left now. Don't miss the trail where it meets the road. Once you get to the brook and cross it you have the option of going straight

160

at first, but then stay left again. This is just through the woods. You may prefer to walk along the river on the left.

Curtis Crossing Dam   Indian Head Reservoir

Tucker Preserve Trail

9b.   Tucker-Luddam's Ford

Directions and parking
Rt. 3 to exit 12 West on Rt. 139 to Rt. 53 south. After ~ 1 mile, turn right at the light
onto Rt. 14. After 1 ½ miles turn right onto Oldham Street After ¾ mile right onto
W. Elm. Go 2 miles to Luddam's Ford Park, the dam, and Tucker Preserve on right.
Park in parking lots on either side of the dam.
 Approximate GPS address 490 West Elm Street, Pembroke, MA

Features
Indian Head River, Luddam's Ford, Tucker Conservation Area
Forest, river, rock formations
that is embedded in the wall on a bridge that crosses the river. The plaque says:
"The Bay Path The Tucker Preserve on the Indian Head River, a tributary of the
North River, maintained by Wildlands Trust, can be enjoyed on foot or by canoe.
Protected land on both sides of the river ensures the canoeist or kayaker a scenic trip.
Near the west side of the preserve, the river quickly winds through a hemlock grove
before it slows and widens downstream, where deep, red cardinal flowers and
basking turtles may be seen.
The Indian Head River is located on the Hanover, Pembroke border in
Massachusetts, United States, and covers about 8 acres (32,000 m^2). It was probably
a fishing and travel spot for Wompatuck Indians.
The river runs through the Luddams Ford Park named after a guide, James Luddam,
who in 1632 carried Governor Winthrop across the river to get to Weymouth,
Massachusetts. In November 1873, Eugene H. Clapp bought the Old Forge Property
from George Curtis and built the Clapp Rubber Factory on the river. The factory is
no longer there, but the mercury pollution from the factory still clings to the rocks
and fish making it unsafe to drink the water and eat the fish. There is a strip of rubber
along the river on the Pembroke side which people may bounce on.

162

The river now has a manmade dam and fish ladder. The river is stocked with trout. It also has a small beaver population. For two weeks during the summer, the herring run upstream to spawn. If herring are caught they must be released and no motor boats are allowed. Once a year, the Hanover Police hold a free fishing derby for anybody that has a fishing license and a fishing rod.

There is a plaque at Luddam's Ford across the Indian Head River the boundary line between Pembroke and Hanover 1632 Gov. Winthrop crossed here on the back of James Luddam, his Guide. Site of Saw Mill 1693 Bardin Iron Works 1704 Curtis Anchor Works 1791. Anchor for the Warship Constitution made here in 1797. A Grist Mill 1832 Carding Mill 1839 Clapp Rubber Co. 1873"

Difficulty
3.6 miles; 1:50 hrs. Some short hills

Along Indian Head River

Hike
Start on the north side of the dam. Follow the trail up river staying left. After about 3/4 miles the trail emerges on Water Street, by an abandoned rail road terminal. Parts are used as a residence. Pass the building and pick up the trail again on the left. Follow the trail till it is interrupted by a house, pass around it and then continue the trail on the left. It emerges on Broadway. Turn left and then left again on State St. After you cross the bridge/dam the trail continues on the left again. It meanders along the river. Stay left but continue to use the main trail. Should you be diverted to the left and the river, make your way back to the main trail. After little more than ¼ mile there will be a wide stone path that can take you to the river, but is a dead end. About 500 feet after that you'll cross Rocky Run and then find a trail off to the right. Should you continue straight along the river you'll dead end at a small scenic

163

waterfall. Turn right and then after about 500 feet, take the first trail to the left. Stay left through the woods. You will come to another brook. It is generally dry in the summer and crossable almost anywhere. Should there be too much water, there is a crossing about 500 feet up the brook from the river. After crossing continue the trail east near the river all the way back to the Tucker Conservation Area parking lot. You will pass some interesting rock formations in and out of the river and you will see a small gorge just east of the old railroad station.

Tucker-Luddam's Ford Trail

10.   Willow Brook and Fleetwood Farm Preserves

These two preserves are very well maintained by Wildlands Trust and the trails are marked.
Directions and parking
Take Rt. 3 to Exit 12 West on Rt. 139.Turn left onto Rt. 53 south; then after ~1-mile turn right onto Rt. 14. West. Preserve entrance and parking will be ½ mile on right.

Approximate GPS street address: 100 Barker Street, Pembroke, MA
Hike Difficulty
About 3 miles, mostly flat

Features
Wood boardwalks; Pudding Brook; wood and stone gates; lookout tower; meadows and woods

The Hike
Follow the trail about halfway down the meadow. There will be a trail off to the right. Go by the Harry and Mary Todd Trail marker. The trail will take a slight right and then go over a bridge over pudding Brook. After the bridge go right, but then stay to your left as you go around the circle and return to the bridge passing through meadows, woods and going along the brook. Re-cross the bridge and go back to the meadow. There turn right or north and then follow the trail. It will turn west and then southwest. Eventually it reaches a wooden lookout tower that gives an excellent view of the green expanse of several preserves. Continue on the trail staying to your right until you reach the meadow where you turn right again and head towards the parking area.

Stone Gate

Lookout Tower

Wooden trail

Wooden Gate

165

Frank Werny

Willow Brook and Fleetwood Farm Preserves Trail

IX.   South of Plymouth County (Bourne, Sagamore, Sandwich, Wareham)
1. Beal Preservation Area, Bourne
2. Bourne Farm Wing Pond
3. Cape Cod Canal, Bournedale Hill trail
4. Cape Cod Canal to Sandwich Boardwalk
5. Four Ponds Conservation Area, Bourne
6. Great Neck Conservation Area
7. Theodore Lyman Reservation
8. Sandy Neck Beach.
9. Scorton Creek

166

Distribution of Hikes

1. Beal Preservation Area, Bourne

Directions and parking
Go south on Rt. 3. To exit 1. Merge onto Scenic Hwy/US-6   0.9 mi
Slight right at Herring Pond Rd   0.2 mi. Turn left onto Bournedale Rd.
Beale Preservation Area is on right.
Approximate GPS street address: 20 Bournedale Road, Bourne, MA

Hike Difficulty
About 2.5 miles, 1:20 hrs. several steep ups and downs.

Features
Herring Pond; Herring River; Beal Preservation Park; Indian Cemetery.
Great Herring Pond[4] is a 376-acre (1.5 km^2) warm water pond mostly located in
Plymouth, with the southern portion extending into Bourne. The village of Pondville
in the Cedarville section of Plymouth lies on the eastern shore of the pond. The pond

167

has an average depth of 20 ft (6 m) and a maximum depth of 42 ft (13 m). The bottom is composed of sand, rubble, and muck. A tire reef was installed in 1979 to provide additional fish shelter. The inflow comes from Little Herring Pond, and the outflow goes into the Herring River in Bourne. The Public Access Board gravel ramp in Bourne enters shallow water and is therefore best suited for canoes, inflatable and other shallow-draft, hand-carried craft.
Bournedale Herring Pond Indian Cemetery up to 1880:
(http://www.capecodgravestones.com/mashher.html)

The Hike
From the parking lot cross the wooden bridge in the northwest corner. Follow the path for 1/8 of a mile. There will be a trail to the left into the woods and then uphill. Follow it till it splits near the top of the hill. Take the left fork. Follow it to the dead end and turn around. Now follow the trail north to the power lines (PLs). There go east a few feet and look for the trail on the other side of the power lines. Follow it to another set of PLs. Cross over directly and continue on the trail to Sandy Pond Road. Turn right. A ¼ mile down the road on the right will be the Native American cemetery with access and a view of Great Herring Pond. To return retrace your steps till you get to the now second set of PLs. Turn right and head down the hill. Watch your step. Slippery loose sand! At the bottom, you can proceed straight for a view of the Herring River or just make a right down the trail and head back to the car. You may want to look around at the Beal Preservation Park Area with the remnants of an ax mill and the fish ladder.

Metal remnant from axe mill   Fish ladder

Beal Preservation Trail

2.   Bourne Farm Wing Pond

Direction
Take RT-3 S toward Cape Code/Provincetown.
Take exit #1A/Buzzards Bay/Falmouth onto Scenic Hwy (US-6) toward Buzzards
Bay/Falmouth - go 3.8 mi. At rotary, stay right and take second exit. Take ramp onto
RT-25 E toward RT-28 S/ Falmouth /The Islands and go over the Bourne Bridge. Go
½ way around the rotary at bottom of the bridge and take Rt. 28 South to Falmouth.

Stay on this road until the next Rotary and again go ½ way around the rotary and continue South on Rt. 28. Take the second exit, the exit sign is for West Falmouth, Thomas Landers Rd. At bottom of Exit ramp go right onto Thomas Landers Rd. The street will End in front of you at Rt. 28A, also known as West Falmouth Hwy. Take a right and then an immediate left into the driveway.

There is a mail Box with the number 6 on it at the beginning of the driveway.

Approximate GPS Directions: 6 N Falmouth Hwy, Falmouth, MA

Features

Bourne Farm, Wing Pond Area, Shining Sea Bike Path, Cattle Tunnel, Crocker Pond, Herring Run

Difficulty

2.3 miles, 1 hr.; some short steep hills.

Hike

Park to the right as you pull off the road. Follow the dirt road to the second parking lot. Crocker Pond will be on the left. Then take the nature trail to the cattle tunnel. After passing under the bike path, through the cattle tunnel, take a diagonal left. This is the Big Loop trail. Follow it, staying left, going west first, then north and then east. At the next major intersection, follow the Herring Run signs. After about ¼ mile, the trail merges with a trail coming from the right. There is a sign labeled "Water". Don't take that, but you might explore it. Further west there will be a slightly larger trail to the right taking you to the water and a bridge across. Again, follow the trail to your left to Herring Run, not the one to the Bogs. When you get to Herring Run, cross over and stay to your right. When you get to the bog area, on the left stay left, hike around the bog, and then go to the right of the small pump station on Wing Pond. Follow along the south shore of Wing Pond to the left of the bog, past the parking area to the bike path. Turn right/ south on the path. Then after little more than ¼ mile look for a horse crossing and a bulletin board on the left. This is the North West corner of Bourne Farm. Enter and make you way back along the open field to the car.

Cattle Tunnel   Wing Pond

170

Herring Run   Crocker Pond

Bourne Farm- Wing Pond Trail

171

Frank Werny

Bourne Farm Map

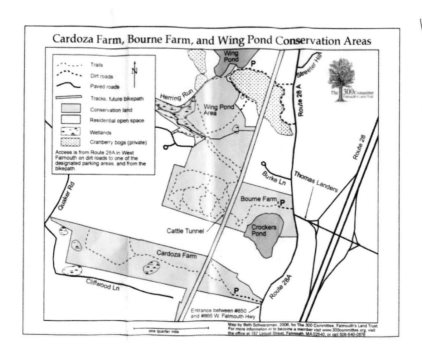

3.　　Cape Cod Canal, Bournedale Hill trail

Directions and parking
Take RT. 3 south to Exit 1A. Bear left towards Rt. 6 and Bourne.
Proceed about 1 mile to a set of lights allowing entrance to the Visitors Center Parking lot. Park there.
Approximate GPS street address: 850 Scenic Hwy, Bourne, MAS

Hike Difficulty
3.31 miles; 1:10 hrs. almost flat

Features:
Cape Cod Canal Herring River fish ladder; quiet walk in woods and walk along the canal; sea birds and an occasional snake.

172

Bourne Bridge, with Railroad Bridge in distance

Cape Cod Canal[4] is a man-made waterway traversing the narrow neck of land that joins Cape Cod to mainland Massachusetts.

Part of the Atlantic Intracoastal Waterway, the canal is roughly 17.4 miles long (approximately 7 of which are cut through land)[1] and connects Cape Cod Bay in the north to Buzzards Bay in the south. The 540-foot width of the canal is spanned by the Cape Cod Canal and two highway bridges -- the Bourne and the Sagamore. Traffic lights govern the approach of vessels over 65 feet, and are located at either end of the canal.

Early History

The idea of constructing such a canal was first considered by Miles Standish of the Plymouth in 1623, and Pilgrims scouted the low-lying stretch of land between the Manomet and the Scusset rivers for potential routes. William Bradford established the trading post of Aptuxcet in 1627 at the portage between the rivers. Trade with the Native Americans of Narragansett Bay and the Dutch of New Netherlands prospered and was a major factor enabling the Pilgrims to pay off their indebtedness. In 1697, the General Court of Massachusetts considered the first formal proposal to build the canal, but apparently took no action. More energetic planning with surveys took place repeatedly in 1776 (by George Washington), 1791, 1803, 1818, 1824-1830, and 1860. None of these efforts came to fruition. The first attempts at actually building a canal did not take place until the late 19th century; earlier planners either ran out of money or were overwhelmed by the project's size.

Canal engineers first needed to understand the theory of plate tectonics, because when the continents came together the bedrock was changed as a result. They needed to know what kind of bedrock they were dealing with. The engineers finally decided which route through the hillsides to take by connecting and widening the Manomet and Scusset Rivers.

The *Gov. Warfield* digging the canal in 1914

Digging the canal
On June 22, 1909, construction finally began for a working canal under the direction of August Belmont, Jr.'s Boston, Cape Cod & New York Canal Company, using designs by engineer William Barclay Parsons. There were many problems that the engineers of the canal encountered; one was mammoth sized boulders. Divers were hired to blow them up, but the effort slowed dredging. Another problem was cold winter storms, which forced the engineers to stop dredging altogether and wait for spring. Nevertheless, the canal opened on a limited basis in 1914, and was completed in 1916.

The Hike
From parking lot proceed south past the Visitor Center, then past the fish ladder. Then there is a sign and staircase to the beginning of the trail. Follow the wooded trail for about 1.5 miles to the RV camp. Once in the RV camp, turn left and look for stairs down to the path along the canal. Turn left or north and return to the Visitors Center and parking area.

Tug Boat   Fish ladder

Bournedale Hill Trail

4.   **Cape Cod Canal to Sandwich Boardwalk**

Directions and parking
Take Rt.3 across Sagamore Bridge, then take Exit 1 and go north on Rt. 6A towards
Sandwich. After about 2 miles, make a left onto Tupper Road and then a left onto
Freezer Road. Then make a right onto Ed Moffitt Drive and another right onto Canal
Service Road, which ends at the Canal Visitors Center.
Approximate GPS street address: Canal Service Rd, Sandwich, MA

Hike Difficulty
The hike is about 4 miles and may take 1 ½ hours. It is flat but walking on the beach
can be difficult for some.

Features
Beach; marshes; boardwalk. Cape Cod Canal; A nice walk along the Canal, the
beach, beach community and beach woods.

The Hike
From the Canal side of the parking lot take the road east towards the end of the
Canal. Turn right on the beach and follow it past the homes on the right to the end of
the beach. Turn around and take the boardwalk on the left. Take the boardwalk till
you can turn right to the parking lot. Follow the parking lot and then the street. Make
a right onto Freeman Avenue and follow it to the end, where you will find a

restaurant parking lot. In the northwest corner of the parking lot, a small trail will take you through a wooded area parallel to the beach and after you emerge back to the Canal. Now you head southwest along the Canal back to the parking lot.

Salt Marsh

Sandwich Board Walk

Sandwich Beach

Northern end of Canal

Sandwich Board Walk
5.   **Four Ponds Conservation Area, Bourne**

Directions
Take the Rt. -3 south. Go 8 miles across Sagamore Bridge.
After Sagamore Bridge, take exit 1C toward Sagamore/MA-6A
Merge onto Mid Cape Connector. Go 0.2 miles. Turn left at MA-6A/Sandwich Rd.
Go 3 miles. At Bourne Bridge Rotary Circle take the 4th exit onto General
MacArthur Blvd/MA-28. Go 3.4 miles. Slight right onto Barlow's Landing
Rd/Pocasset-Forestdale Rd. Continue to follow Barlow's Landing Rd. 0.7 miles.
Park on right.
Approximate GPS address 142 Barlow's Landing Rd, Pocasset or Bourne, MA
02559

Features
Mill Pond; Shop Pond; The Basin; Freeman Pond; Upper Pond All four are part of
the beginning of Pocasset River which flows into Buzzards Bay
The Pocasset River is a small, tidal river and estuary on the eastern shore of
Buzzards Bay, in Bourne on Cape Cod. The river flows westward through wetlands
with a total length of about 1 km.
The river's Mill and Shop Ponds were sites for the Pocasset Iron Foundry (1822-81)
and Tahanto Art Works (1882-1900), which made use of the native bog iron. In 1980
it was designated an Area of Critical Environmental Concern by the Massachusetts
Executive Office of Environmental Affairs. Alewife spawn during April and May,
and the river contains bluefish, flounder, scup, striped bass, blue crab, lobster, and
soft-shell clams.

Difficulty
4.2 miles; 2 hrs; some short hills

Hike
From the parking lot stay to your left. When you get to the ponds cross the bridge
between Freeman and Upper Ponds. Turn left after the bridge. Walk along Freeman
Pond on your left, The Basin on your right, and then Shop Pond on your left. From
here, you can see Mill Pond across the road. Turn around and then go left so that you
will have The Basin to your right. At the northern tip of The Basin, continue
northeast for about ¼ mile. Then look for a trail east that will take you to Pine Trail.
Go left on Pine Trail. It is marked and crosses some fire roads as well as Town
Forest Trail. Either of the 2 trails will bring you full circle through quiet wooded
areas back to the parking lot area. However, it is safest to follow one or the other set
of markers.

Swans on pond   Bridge and pond

Bridge between ponds   Sunning turtles

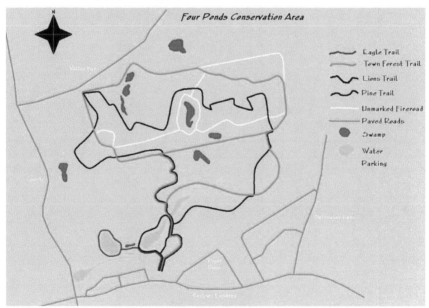

Town Trail Map

Frank Werny

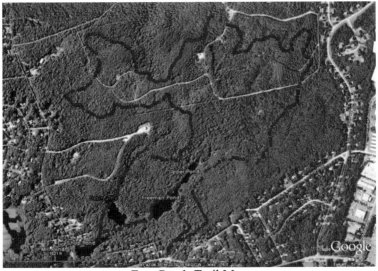

Four Ponds Trail Map

6.   Great Neck Conservation Area

Directions: Take RT-3 S. Exit #1A toward BUZZARDS BAY/FALMOUTH. Continue to follow US-6. At BOURNE ROTARY take second exit ramp onto RT-25 W toward 195/I-495 Then take exit #2/ONSET (US-6)/WAREHAM (RT-28) onto GLEN CHARLIE RD toward ONSET (US-6)/WAREHAM (RT-28) go 0.57 mi. Continue on DEPOT ST go 0.42 mi. Continue on GREAT NECK RD go 1.17 m. Turn Right on CROOKED RIVER RD go 0.15 mi and arrive at 32 CROOKED RIVER RD, on the left.
Approximate GPS address: 32 Crooked River Road, Wareham, MA

Features
Wildlands Trust Conservation Area[1]; Jack's Marsh (25.4 acres) ;Minot-Weld Conservancy (53 acres) ; Mink Cove-Elkins Reservation (25.6 acres)Phillip Saltonstal-Weld Forest. Swan Pond, Griffith Bog, Buzzards Bay
This pine and oak forest was conserved forever in the name of Phillip Saltonstall Weld by his cousin, Eloise Choate, in 1985. The parcel is surrounded by other conservation land, both public and private. The town owns a water main right-of-way which was enlarged and then seeded, providing excellent access into the property[4].

Difficulty
3.9 miles; 1:45 min.; flat

Swan Pond   Buzzards Bay

Hike

After parking cross the barrier and go a few feet and then turn left. Follow the trail between the houses on the left and the marshy area on the right. At the end of the marsh and after a very short steep incline you can see Swan Pond. Turn right or south. When you get to the fence, follow it around the left. Stay right past the house. Just after the little sheep barn, take the trail to the left into the woods. At the first cross trail turn right and follow a fairly straight trail. At the next cross trail make a right and shortly after a left. That will bring you out in a coulder sac. Stay right and take the first dirt road on the right going southwest, not the one that looks like a long drive way, labelled Mink Cove. At the first cross trail make a left and continue till you come out on a dirt road, Bourne Hill Rd.. Go left and just past the first house, go between the first and second house down to Bourne Point Road and follow it to the left till to the driveway at the end with the two stone gate posts Turn left and make your way to a wide strip of grasss going down to the water. You are now looking at the entrance to Little Harbor.

Little Harbor   **Mink Cove**

Turn around and take the trail to the right. After about 100 yards turrn left andgo till you can turn right on Bourne Hill road Follow it past the house where you turned right down to the water earlier, and the look for the trail going right. Con tinue northwest till you get to the fenced area and retrace you steps.At the end of the fence pass between jack's Bog and Swan Pond. Then make a sharp left at the end of the bog and head west back to the car. Don't miss the little turn of towards the car on the right.

180

The following is the Wildlands Trust trail map of the area: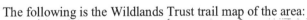

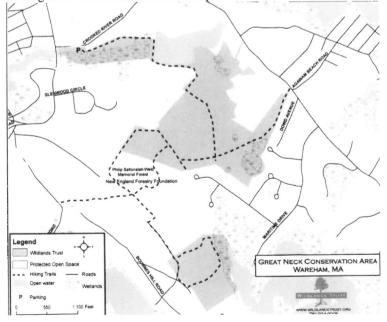

7. Theodore Lyman Reservation

Directions to Theodore Lyman Reservation
From Rt. 3 take exit 1 to Hwy 6 south. At the light Near the Cape Cod Canal Visitors
Center, make a right and then a left onto Bournedale Road. Follow it about two miles
to Head of the Bay Road and make a right. Head of the Bay Road turns into Red
Brook Road. After about 1 ½ miles you pass Packard Street on the right. The parking
lot is 200 feet on the right.
Or
From Rt. 3 Exit 3 take Long Pond Road south to Halfway Pond Road. After a little
less than a mile turn left onto Bourne Road and follow it about 10 miles. When it
ends, turn right. After about 1 mile pass Packard Street on the right and then the
parking lot will be about 200 feet on the right.
Or
From Route 25, get off at exit 3 (to Buzzards Bay, Bourne) just north of the Bourne
Bridge on the Cape Cod Canal. Bear right off ramp and take an immediate right onto
Head of the Bay Road. Follow for approximately three miles around the eastern and
northern shores of Buttermilk Bay. Parking lot entrance is about 250 feet beyond
Packard Street on right.
Approximate GPS address: 98 Red Brook Rd, Wareham, MA

Difficulty
2.8 miles, 1:40 hrs. relatively flat, some short hills

Features
Buttermilk Bay, Red Brook
In addition to Red Brook, the Lyman Reserve features freshwater wetlands, forested
uplands, a sandy beach, and a scenic stretch of coastal shoreline with views of
Buttermilk Bay and the Cape Cod Canal vertical lift railroad bridge.
Red Brook, the ecological, cultural, and scenic highlight of the reservation, is a 4.5-
mile, spring-fed, coldwater stream that flows from White Island Pond to Buttermilk
Bay. One of the few coastal streams in Massachusetts that supports anadromous fish
(migratory fish which hatch in freshwater, make their way to sea to grow, and return
as adults to spawn), Red Brook is home to one the last remaining native sea-run
brook trout fisheries in the eastern United States. It was one family's love for these
"salters" that made the preservation of this special place possible.
From: http://www.thetrustees.org/places-to-visit/southeast-ma/lyman-reserve.html

The Hike
The trail starts in the northwest corner of the parking lot. Follow the trail to the first
trail to the left. Take a detour to the left for a view of Red Brook. Return to the main
trail and continue to the bridge. Cross and continue uphill into the open area. When
you reach the first trail to the right follow it. When you reach the wooded area do not
go right. Continue straight. Continue to a water company building. Go past the
building and then fine the trail just to the left. You will come to another building.

Take the trail just to the right of the building. At the road junction stay right and follow the trail all the way to Hwy 25. Turn around. When you get back to the several road junction take the trail slightly to your left. It will take you down to the river. Follow the trail south along the brook to the area marked New Bridge on the maps. There is no bridge. From the brook go west up the hill and emerge in the open area again. Go left and then left again. This will take you back to the first bridge you crossed. Turn right after the bridge and return to the parking lot. Cross the parking lot. Take the trail to the road. The trail continues across the street a few feet left of the drive way. Continue on the trail till it splits, stay left and find yourself on the shore of Buttermilk Bay. Follow the shore to the right and complete the circle. Turn left and go back to the parking lot across the street.

Railroad Bridge, Buttermilk Bay and Red Brook

Red Brook Out flow   Bridge over Red Brook

Lyman Trail Map

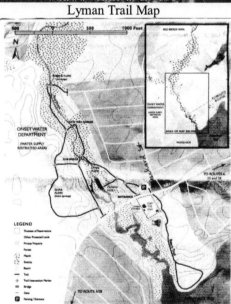

http://www.thetrustees.org/assets/documents/places-to-visit/trailmaps/Lyman-Trail-Map.pdf

8.   Sandy Neck Beach.

Directions and parking
Take Rt.3 south across Sagamore Bridge. Take Exit 1 and follow signs to Rt. 6A (Sandwich). Follow Rt. 6A past Sandwich just over the town line in East Sandwich to Sandy Neck Road on left. Follow Sandy Neck Road to the beach parking lot. Memorial Day to Labor Day Town of Sandwich residents parking only.
Approximate GPS Address: 99 Sandy Neck Rd, Sandwich, MA

Hike Difficulty
The hike can be 8 miles or less. 2:40hrs. or less; Walking is difficult at times because of loose sand on the south side of the dunes and beach on the north side varies from hard sand to loose gravel. No hills though.

Features
Beautiful walk between dunes and salt marshes on the way out and a long walk on the beach with the water on one and the dunes on the other side. Cape Cod bay, Dunes, Intra-dunal areas; great salt marshes; Beach Point; 4miles of beach.
Sandy Neck, a coastal barrier beach, is approximately six miles long, varying in width from 200 yards to one half mile. This unique conservation and recreation area is owned by the Town of Barnstable and is under the supervision and jurisdiction of the Town Manager, with the advice of Sandy Neck Board. Help preserve and protect the heritage and integrity of this resource.
http://town.barnstable.ma.us/Conservation/TrailGuides/HikersGuides/Sandy%20Nec k%20Brochure4client.pdf . Gatehouse Hours: 508-362-8300. 8:00a.m. to 9p.m

The Hike
From parking lot go south a few feet and take the dirt/sand road, Marsh Trail, to the left. Do not take trail #1. Marsh Trail will follow the south side of the dunes for about 4 miles to Beach Point. Crossover to the beach is possible in several places. Going out, there will be great marshes on your right and dunes on the left with many interesting intra-dunal areas. If you go all the way to the end your round trip will be about 8 miles of hard walking on a sandy road and the return on the beach can vary from loose sand to rocks to gravel.

Dunal areas

185

Salt Marsh   Sandy Neck Beach

Sandy Neck Beach Trail

9.   Scorton Creek

Directions

Take State Rt. 3 across Sagamore Bridge. Go to exit 3, head left off ramp towards East Sandwich.

Turn right at Rt. 6A. Go just past Pine Terrace on right. Make right into State Game Farm, just before marsh area and bridge. Go south past the hatchery entrance till you dead end at a parking area.

Approximate GPS address is 515 Rt-6A or Cranberry Hwy, East Sandwich, MA.

Features

Scorton Creek Marshes; Scorton Creek; Hoxie Pond, Talbot's Point Conservation Lands; MA East Sandwich Game Farm: http://www.thorntonburgess.org/EastSandwichGameFarm.htm

Difficulty
3.8 miles; 1:40 hrs. flat

Hike
From the parking lot continue on the road till you get to a trail map on the left. Here turn left and follow the trail staying left. There are some short excursions to the marsh from the trail. Come back to the trail and stay left. You will cross a bridge and then come to an intersection. Turn left again and follow the trail along the north edge of the field. Just past the field on the right turn right and follow the trail to another intersection. Here turn left and go across a smaller bridge. Turn left again and stay left. Follow the trail around this little peninsula till you come back to the intersection where you originally turned left. Turn left again, cross the bridge and turn left again. Now head south till you get to Old County Line Road. There will be a small parking lot on the right, and then you will cross the railroad tracks, and then Old County Line Road. Turn right and walk along the road for a little over ¼ miles. Pass the houses and a pond on the right and then make a right onto a dirt road. Cross the railroad tracks again, and continue past the field on the right. By the next open area stay left. After crossing the bridge continue and then turn left onto Hoxie Trail. Follow it. It makes a sharp right after about ¼ miles. This will bring you to a small access to Hoxie Pond. Take the trail on the right just before the pond access. Follow the trail about a ¼ mile again, and then you can take a smaller trail on the right or go straight and end up on the road along the marsh and turn right to get to the car.
If you take the smaller trail turn left at the first split and follow the windy trail till you get to the road. Turn left and that will take you back to the car.

Scorton Creek

Sandy Beach at Scorton Creek

Scorton Creek Hike

Index

Made in the USA
Charleston, SC
09 May 2011